Reflections on the Path to Wholeness
Volume 4

CROSSROADS

BRENDA S. JACKSON, PH.D.

Detroit, Michigan, USA

Reflections on the Path to Wholeness, Volume 4: Crossroads
Copyright © 2010 Brenda S. Jackson, Ph.D.

All scripture quotations, unless otherwise indicated, taken from the HOLY BIBLE, NEW INTERNATIONAL VERSION®. NIV®. Copyright© 1973, 1978, 1984 by International Bible Society. Used by permission of Zondervan. All rights reserved.

Scripture quotations marked (KJV) are taken from the HOLY BIBLE, KING JAMES VERSION (Authorized).

All poetry submissions herein are © 2000 – 2010 Brenda S. Jackson

All rights reserved. No part of this publication may be reproduced, stored in a retrieval system, or transmitted in any form or by any means – electronic, mechanical, photocopy, recording, or any other – except for brief quotations in printed reviews, without the prior permission of the publisher.

*Priority*ONE Publications
P. O. Box 725 • Farmington, MI 48332
(800) 596-4490 Nationwide Toll Free
E-mail: info@p1pubs.com
URL: http://www.p1pubs.com

ISBN 13: 978-1-933972-20-6
ISBN 10:   1-933972-20-3

Edited by Patricia A. Hicks
Cover and interior design by PriorityONE Publications

Printed in the United States of America

TABLE OF CONTENTS

Dedication 4
Anointing Prayer by Brenda M. Rudolph..............................5
Seminar #1   I Am Mortal (Faith and Aging)........................7
Seminar #2   The Die is Cast (Decision Making in the Will of God) 41
Seminar #3   Selecting the Easy Yoke (Breaking Yokes).....................59
Seminar #4   Failure of Pride versus Power of Humility 85
Seminar #5   Fruit: Spiritually Sweet, Emotionally Mature 103
Seminar #6   Prayer Power 121
Benediction Elder Arnoldine Lancaster............................150
About the Author 151

DEDICATION

In the name of Jesus and in the power of The Holy Spirit, Volume IV, the last in the series of *"Reflections On The Path To Wholeness"* is written. This journey has drawn me closer to the gospel and the meaning of visiting Jesus in prison and setting the captives free.

It is with sincere thanks that I acknowledge the prayers, assistance, and encouragement of the publisher, editor, the incarcerated, and the volunteers of BSJ Christian Seminars, Inc.

This volume is dedicated to those being paroled, who are committed to living godly lives, and helping in developing better neighborhoods, a better City, a better County, a better State, and ultimately a better America, all in the name and to the glory of Jesus, The Christ.

Dr. Jackson as she enters the prison in Pretoria, South Africa.

ANOINTING PRAYER

Our Most Holy and Gracious Father,
We come before your throne of grace dedicating this book to those who are facing life's challenges and seeking divine guidance and direction. We pray that you speak through the contents of each chapter of this book that you transform lives from mortality to immortality; from hopelessness to a life empowered through Christ Jesus.

We thank you Lord, by faith for the blessings, healing and deliverance as you speak through the pages of this book. Amen.

                                                           Sister Brenda M. Rudolph

CROSSROADS
© Brenda Simuel Jackson

We enter life at a crossroad with arrows pointing in the direction where we grow.

Sometimes we have loving help to get us over all roadblocks, and keep us growing in the right direction wherever we go.

Sometimes we are dumped on the curb, and left to die, or live as best we can.

Having gotten past the crossroads of puberty, peer pressure, drugs, and sex, making right and wrong choices, not allowing self to find what is really the best.

Finally we accept that we must choose life or death for ourselves, we must repent and believe or deny and not receive our reprieve.

Which road will we follow? Jesus said, "Come my yoke is easy and my burdens are light." He said, "Come, and I will give you rest."

Choose the road that leads to eternal life, the road of Jesus Christ is the road that provides life's best.

Chapter 1
I AM MORTAL

Faith and Aging

BSJ Christian Seminars
Minister Brenda Simuel Jackson, Ph.D.
© 2004 All rights reserved.

SEMINAR OBJECTIVES

- Identify stages of maturing faith

- Provide assistance in accepting our own mortality

- Identify obstacles to joyful aging

- Improve spiritual coping skills for aging seasons

- Show how to look past mortality to immortality

I AM MORTAL
© Brenda Simuel Jackson[1]

I am mortal, born to die.

I am mortal, body decay is a sign of life.

I am mortal, strength decreases lagging behind my will.

I am mortal, information once gained, I don't always retain.

I am mortal, mortality has lessened my number of friends.

I am mortal, but my future is not grim.

I am mortal, but I have my security deposit for eternal life.

I am mortal, departed friends and family, one day I know I will see.

I am mortal, with everlasting life with Christ is my guarantee.

I am mortal, but that's Okay, Immortality is a gift Christ has given to me.

---

[1] Brenda S. Jackson, *Reflections on the Path to Wholeness: A Journey of Redeeming Faith, Volume 1,* [Detroit, MI: PriorityONE Publications, 2007], 107.

FORWARD

The Book of Ecclesiastes
"Can You Breathe"

Purpose:
To demonstrate or to prove that without God there is no meaning in life.

Theme:
What is the philosophical meaning to life?

Key Verses:
Ecclesiastes 12:13-14
New Testament Cognate: John 14:6

Application:
The Plan of Salvation and receiving eternal life

Historical Context:
The book was written by Solomon (1:1). He may have written the Book during the period near the end of his reign after his wives had turned him from God, and he was lost.[2] The Book may have been written after Solomon's return to God. The reign of Solomon was the last king of Israel, and it was during his reign that the Northern and Southern Kingdoms were established. Idolatry was practiced during Solomon's reign as he permitted his wives to erect shrines, to their gods, which caused his heart not to be fully devoted to God.[3]

Audience:
The original audience appears to be Solomon, himself.

---

[2] J. Vernon McGee, *Thru the Bible with J. Vernon McGee, Vol III*: [Pasadena California: Thru The Bible Radio, 1982], 104.
[3] Lawrence O. Richards, *The Revell Bible Dictionary,* [Old Tappan, New Jersey: Fleming H. Revell Co., 1990], 934.

KEY WORDS AND PHRASES:

Vanity is a key word through out the Book. The Hebrew word is הבל (hebel). The meaning in the context of the book is emptiness, transitory, and/or unsatisfactory.[4]

The root word means vapor or breath; this is the opposite of the word breath as in the Spirit from God; His breath is the breath of life which allows man to breathe and to live, and the Hebrew word is רוּחַ (ruah), which is the same word for Spirit. The breath in Ecclesiastes is transitory, worthless, and causes man to become vain. (an indication of the mortality of man). In the book of Genesis, chapter 4, the Hebrew word for breathe is Abel, Adam's son who was killed by his brother after he (Abel), found favor with God. Cain's sacrifice was worthless in God's sight, and Cain was too vain to do it right. Cain never sought forgiveness for his actions. It is noted that the term Abel is used without explanation and this is different from other names which are described by progenitor or position.[5] In the book of Job, vanity is translated as shortness of life, meaningless life, and nonsense in comfort (Job 7:16; 9:29; 21:34; and 35:16). In Job, the meaning is also associated with idolatry.[6] The word is used to designate the false gods worshipped by the people of God (Deuteronomy 32:21; 1 Kings 16:13, 26; Jeremiah 2:5).[7] This is a descriptor of the period in Solomon's life when he allowed such worship to flourish. When in the context of emptiness and idol worship, the answer to the theme may be that life is empty without our Lord which explains Solomon's search; he is trying to return to God and a meaningful life, as in "ruah".

Another key word throughout the book is the use of the pronoun "**I**". Solomon refers to himself over seventy (70) times between 1:12 and 10:7; whereas in Chapters 11 and 12, he begins to acknowledge God (11:5 and

---

[4] James Strong, *The Exhaustive Concordance of The Bible with Dictionaries of the Hebrew and Greek Words.* [Peabody, Mass: Henderickson Publishers, 2007]. Strong's number 1892.
[5] R. Laird Harris, Gleason L. Archer, Jr. & Bruce K. Waltke, *Theological Wordbook of The Old Testament,* [Chicago, IL, Moody Bible Institute, 1980], 204.
[6] Strong, *The Exhaustive Concordance.*
[7] Harris, *Theological Wordbook.*

12:1) who provides meaning to it all. When referring to himself, alone, all is vanity, e.g. 2:1.

A critical phrase is "Under the Sun." The emphasis is on man's reasoning and things under man's control, as man has dominion over all the earth, Genesis 1:26. The phrase is used over twenty (20) times. This locates man's control only on this earth, not over the universe. The emptiness is on this earth without God.

APPLICATION:
This is a research project conducted by Solomon in his search for meaning in life. Is your life empty? Where are you searching? For what are you searching? Will it last if you find it? Have you found God in your life? The key verses give us the answer and lead us to recognize that our answer is not under the sun, but through the Son:

> Let us hear the conclusion of the whole matter: Fear God, and keep His commandments; for this is the whole duty of man. For God shall bring every work into judgment, with every secret thing, whether it be good, or whether it be evil.
> Ecclesiastes 12:13 KJV

MORTALITY

I. When does meaning in life begin and end? (Ecclesiastes 3:1-8)
    A. There is a Time for every thing.
        1. Time – an appointed fixed period
        2. Appointed by God
        3. Not in reference to an hour or minute of designated time
        4. An opportunity
        5. A season

    B. Solomon says that all activity in life is without true purpose or value. (1:14 – 6:2)
        1. Search for meaning in all things God created (1:14)
        2. Looked at his role as King.
        3. Looked at his wisdom.

        4.   Looked at his accomplishments.
        5.   Looked at his ability to reason.
        6.   Looked at the pleasures in life.

   C.   For every positive in life there appears to be a negative.
        1.   Where there is wisdom, there is sorrow. Example - 1:18
        2.   Where there is knowledge there is grief.

II. Mortality and Aging – Ecclesiastes: 12:1-7
(Discuss each verse)

   A.   v1 Trouble is the synonym for age – Is there pleasure in growing old?

   B.   v2 When sight is dim, need large print, even with the glasses – Is there pleasure?

   C.   v3 When the limbs no longer are mobile enough to do for self and can no longer stand straight – Is there pleasure in life?

   D.   v4 When there is no longer the need to go to work, rise early, but for naught – Is there pleasure?

   E.   v5 Agility is no longer present, hair naturally is white or gray [maybe gone].

   F.   v5 One's future only points to death.

   G.   v6 It is important to remember our creator before death occurs.

   H.   v7 Body will return to dust and the Spirit returns to God who gave it. Where will your spirit go?

THE NATURE OF MAN

I. Life
    A. Man created in God's image (Genesis 1:27, 5:1)

    B. Man created in God's likeness
        1. Man created in God's Spiritual likeness (Genesis 2:7)
        2. God is Spirit (John 4:24)
        3. Life is from God

    C. Man has two components:
        1. Body is made from dust. (Genesis 2:7; 2 Corinthians 5:1)
            a. The body is not in an eternal state
            b. The body dies, returns to dust (Job 10:9, 34:14-15)
            c. The body returns in new state
        2. The Spirit is eternal (Job 34:14-15; Psalm 104:29-30)
        3. The mind of man often seen as third component [8]

---

[8] Harold G. Koenig, M.D. MHsc., *Aging and God,* (New York: Haworth Pastoral Press, 1993) Figure 1, 105-35.

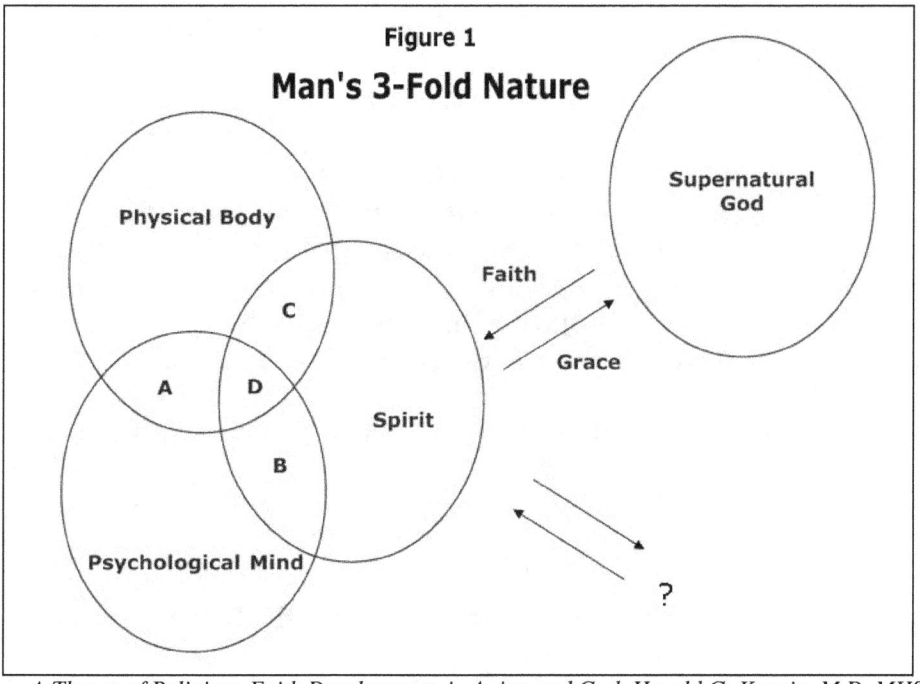

A Theory of Religious Faith Development, in Aging and God, Harold G. Koenig, M.D. MHSc.

    4.   Three natures overlap
        a.   Spirit is the constant state of man
        b.   God is Spirit, interacts with man through the Spirit
        c.   Body of man influences his mind during illnesses
            i.   Alzheimer's
            ii.   Strokes
            iii.   Disease
    5.   Mind may influence body, psychosomatic
    6.   Physical illnesses impact aging prisoners (Aday, 126, 192)
        a.   Arthritis
        b.   Heart Disease
        c.   Emphysema
        d.   Strokes

       e.   Studies of female inmates indicate special needs:
   - i. Depression
   - ii. Menopause
   - iii. Osteoporosis
   - iv. Degenerative bone condition
7. Through the Spirit, God affects mind and body
   - a. Spirit influences emotions
   - b. Spirit influences motivation
   - c. Spirit affects cognitive (behavioral) processes.
8. Faith determines if channels open between God and man's spirit
9. The eternal part of man (James 2:26; Job 34:14-15; Psalm 104:29; Hebrews 12:9)
   - a. Spirit of God is in man (Romans 8:9, 29)
   - b. The Spirit of Christ in the Believer (Romans 8:9, 29)
   - c. The Glory of the Lord in man is the Spirit of the Lord (2 Corinthians 3:18)
   - d. Man's personality traits from his spirit
     - i. Self-consciousness
     - ii. Self-determination
     - iii. Making choices
   - e. Man can be redeemed because of his spirit.
   - f. There is a future life.

Discussion Questions:

Our seasons in life change as we mature, grow older, and our faith should mature also. If we evaluate our maturity by our chronological age, can we also evaluate the maturity of our faith by the same measure, or can we evaluate faith's maturity by the level of truths guiding the seasons of our life?

Psalm 90:10 (NIV) says, " the length of our days is seventy or eighty, if we have the strength; yet their span is but trouble, and sorrow for they quickly pass, and we fly away." At this season in life, the body is mature; does our faith match the maturity we have achieved in age?

> *"Concerning this we have much to say which is hard to explain, since you have become dull in your [spiritual] hearing and sluggish [even slothful in achieving spiritual insight]. For even though by this time you ought to be teaching others, you actually need someone to teach you over again the very first principles of God's Word. You have come to need milk, not solid food. For everyone who continues to feed on milk is obviously inexperienced and unskilled in the doctrine of righteousness (of conformity to the divine will in purpose, thought, and action), for he is a mere infant [not able to talk yet]. But solid food is for full grown men, for those whose senses and mental faculties are trained by practice to discriminate and distinguish between what is morally good and noble, and what is evil and contrary either to divine or human law. Therefore let us go on and get past the elementary stage in the teachings and doctrine of Christ (the Messiah), advancing steadily toward completeness and perfection that belong to spiritual maturity."*
>
> Hebrew 5:11-6:1a AMP

Are we blessed to reach ages of 50, 60, 70, 80+, having confessed Christ, and claimed the family of Christ for 10, 20, 30, 50+ years, but we still are on milk and not solid foods, not knowing the truths which sustain us in all situations? Are we as Solomon's research proved, and his poem in Ecclesiastes 3:1-8 says, left the truths of God, and therefore, all is vanity, empty, and our spiritual maturity is as a vapor?

MATURING FAITH

I. Growing Spiritually in Faith:
    A. Believing
    B. Experiencing
    C. Acting

II. Promise based on relationship with higher being (Hebrew 11:1 – 12:2)

III. Trust and faith in God provide mental stability to overcome loss (Pastoral Care, Koenig & Weaver).

IV. Ages according to Gerontology:
- Young/Old ages 65 –74
- Aged – ages 75 –84
- Oldest old– ages 85+

ECCLESIASTES 3:1-8

BEGINNING SEASONS	SEASON OF LIVING	ENDING SEASON	A NEW BEGINNING
A time of birth	Aging: 0-20 21-40 41-60 61-80 81+ ___ ___ ___ ___ ___ Spiritual Maturity: 0-20 21-40 41-60 61-80 81+ ___ ___ ___ ___ ___	A time to die	John 3:16 2 Corinthians 5:8 1 Corinthians 15:22-23 1 Thessalonians 4:16
A time to plant (for food)	Aging: 0-20 21-40 41-60 61-80 81+ ___ ___ ___ ___ ___ Spiritual Maturity: 0-20 21-40 41-60 61-80 81+ ___ ___ ___ ___ ___	A time to uproot, no longer grow	Revelation 22:2
A time to kill (death and destruction)	Aging: 0-20 21-40 41-60 61-80 81+ ___ ___ ___ ___ ___ Spiritual Maturity: 0-20 21-40 41-60 61-80 81+ ___ ___ ___ ___ ___	A time to heal (weeping and mourning)	Revelation 22:3
A time to tear down, scatter stones; (time to build anew, relocate)	Aging: 0-20 21-40 41-60 60-80 81+ ___ ___ Spiritual Maturity: 0-20 21-40 41-60 60-80 81+ ___ ___ ___ ___ ___	A time to gather (in the family tombs, the bones were gathered together and placed in a box to make room for others)	John 14:1-4

BEGINNING SEASONS	SEASON OF LIVING	ENDING SEASON	A NEW BEGINNING
A time to weep, A time to mourn	Aging: 0-20 21-40 41-60 61-80 81+ ___ ___ ___ ___ ___ Spiritual Maturity: 0-20 21-40 41-60 61-80 81+ ___ ___ ___ ___ ___	A time to laugh (death brings release, Job 3:21-22) A time to dance	Revelation 22:3 Revelation 21:4 Isaiah 65:17-19
A time to scatter stones; A time to embrace	Aging: 0-20 21-40 41-60 61-80 81+ ___ ___ ___ ___ ___ Spiritual Maturity: 0-20 21-40 41-60 61-80 81+ ___ ___ ___ ___ ___	A time to gather stones; a time to refrain from embracing (there is a time to stop building, even relationships)	Revelations 21:3 Mark 12:25
A time to search; A time to keep	Aging: 0-20 21-40 41-60 61-80 81+ ___ ___ ___ ___ ___ Spiritual Maturity: 0-20 21-40 41-60 61-80 81+ ___ ___ ___ ___ ___	A time to give up; A time to throw away (things are no longer of great importance.)	
A time to tear; a time to be silent (as one in mourning, those who sat with Job, those who tear their clothes in mourning)	Aging: 0-20 21-40 41-60 61-80 81+ ___ ___ ___ ___ ___ Spiritual Maturity: 0-20 21-40 41-60 61-80 81+ ___ ___ ___ ___ ___	A time to mend and a time to speak (mourning is no more)	Revelation 21:1,2

A time for hate; A time for war (hostilities)	Aging: 0-20 21-40 41-60 61-80 81+ ___ ___ ___ ___ ___ Spiritual Maturity: 0-20 21-40 41-60 61-80 81+ ___ ___ ___ ___ ___	A time for love and a time for peace	Revelation 22:1-5,14

Read Psalm 90:8-17 and 34:8-12
Copy the above chart and make handouts. Each participant is to determine where they are on the scale of life and faith. Discuss the results.

Arguments:
- Application of faith and God's truths produce a better life and is profitable to God.
- Grace is superior to dead works.
- Understanding leads to godly living.

Scriptures: Hebrew 5:11 – 6:20; Key Scriptures: 5:1-10
I.   Jesus made perfect [salvation] through His suffering.
    A.   Perfect – reached its end, finished
        1.   Perfect in age
        2.   Complete in goodness

    B.   Source of eternal salvation:
        1.   Source of all who obey
        2.   Chosen by God as High Priest-order of Melchizedek
            a.   Dual office
                i.   Priest
                ii.   King
            b.   Psalm 2:7 "I will proclaim the decree of the Lord He said to me, 'You are my son, today I have become Your Father'" (Jesus' appointment)

     i. Davidic kingdom (Act 4:25)
     ii. Psalm 22 – Suffering Servant (part of trilogy)
  C. Experientially, God acquired knowledge of human condition.

II. v. 11 We have much to say about the order of Melchizedek:
  A. Term used for teacher is same term used when referring to Jesus as Teacher.

  B. How long is one a babe in Christ:
   1. Romans 14:1 –22:
    a. What a person can eat
    b. What a person thinks is sin
    c. One easily made weaker in the faith
   2. The elementary things:
    a. Repenting from acts leading to death
     i. Depending on works which cannot save
     ii. Allowing self to practice sin
    b. Note: Salvation based on Faith – Stand
     i. (James) Works do not save – note later what is true fruit.
     ii. Jesus is the Author and Finisher of our Faith (Yesua), no longer worry, demonstrates love
    c. Instructions in baptism
     i. Matthew 28:19-20 (Great Commission)
     ii. Baptism in time of Jesus, ritual of personal purification required by the law (John's baptism)
    d. Laying on of hands, not that of healing but that of Acts 8:17:
     i. Sign of receiving Holy Spirit after Apostles laid on hands
     ii. Anointing
     iii. A commission, ordination
     iv. Showing a blessing, a setting aside

   e. Baptism is symbolization (under the law) of repentance
   f. Resurrection of the dead -
    i. O.T resurrection only in Daniel 12:2 – "Multitudes who sleep in the dust of the earth will awake; some to everlasting life, others to shame and everlasting contempt." (NIV)
    ii. N.T distinguishes between resurrection of believer and non-believer (1 Thessalonians 4:13-18)
    iii. 1 John 3:1-3 Believers are to be like Christ, a Hope; purified because He purifies

III. v5:13 Maturity – Teachings for living/dying
 A. O.T righteousness, an absolute quality of God (Psalm 4:1; Jeremiah 12:1)
  1. Jeremiah 12:1 – Righteousness related to judgment
  2. Righteousness of God is His faithfulness
  3. Righteousness is a quality which must condemn sin.
  4. Righteousness conforms to the will of God.
 B. Righteous, a gift received from God resulting from faith in Jesus Christ
  1. Righteousness is not by obeying the Law
  2. Man's merit cannot attain righteousness
  3. Exercised faith brings right standing (Romans 4:6, 11: sign of circumcision – seal of righteousness that Abraham had by faith while still uncircumcised)
  4. 2 Corinthians 5:21 – Faith brings righteousness
  5. Romans 14:23b – Everything not from faith is from sin

IV. Perseverance (v14)
 A. Hypothetical argument (If it is falling away, then salvation cannot be attained; Salvation is attained; therefore, it is not falling away)

1. Impossible (no probability allowed):
   a. Spiritually in the light
   b. Tasted the heavenly gift
      i. Blessings of faith
      ii. Blessings of righteousness
      iii. Spirit filled
2. Goodness of Word of God (Psalm 119:97-106)
   a. Wiser than enemies
   b. More insight than teacher
   c. More understanding than elders
3. Power of the coming age
   a. Eternal life – Mark 10:30
   b. Current age – homes, families, fields
4. The question – Are we trying to re-crucify Christ?

B. v6:1 Crucifixion deterrence of others from certain crimes:
   1. Christ, High Priest, not again crucified
   2. Failure to live in faith, apply truth, a disgrace to Christ
   3. Can crucify Christ through wrong actions

C. v6:7 We are branches, Christ is the Vine (John 15:5-6)
   1. Prune – vine grows
   2. Prune – vine bears fruit
   3. No pruning – no real fruit grows
   4. Fruit must be usuable
   5. Question – Is God using your fruit?
   6. The useless is thrown away – cursed

D. v6:9 What accompanies salvation?
   1. Reconciliation back to God (Romans 5:10; Colossians 1:21-22, 2 Corinthians 5:18-19)
   2. Atonement through Christ (Hebrew 2:17)
   3. Forgiveness (Ephesians 2:7, 1:7)
   4. Justification – receiving righteousness (Romans 5:1)
   5. Regeneration (John 3:3-6, 2 Corinthians 5:17 – new nature)

        6.   Security (Ephesians 1:4-5)
        7.   Adoption by God (Galatians 4:5, Romans 8:15)
        8.   Sanctification – Separated from evil (1 Thessalonians 4:3)

    E.   Application
        1.   Obedient to God's will
        2.   Knowing God's promises
        3.   Receiving God's promises

IV.   God is a just God
    A.   God's attributes
        1.   Just
        2.   Perfect agreement between God's nature and His acts (John 17:25; Romans 3:26)
            a.   Righteous
            b.   Actions demonstrate His justice
            c.   Faithful (1 John 1:9 – if we confess…He is faithful)

    B.   Perseverance
        1.   Add to your faith
        2.   Live godly (2 Peter 1:5)

    C.   Blessings of perseverance
        1.   Persevering during difficult times
        2.   Aging
        3.   Ecclesiastes 5:19-6:2b
            a.   Ability to enjoy possessions
            b.   Contentment with lot
            c.   Happy in work
            d.   Gladness of heart
            e.   Unable to enjoy blessings

THEORY STAGES OF FAITH (KOENIG)[9]

I. Early Childhood (Ages 0-2)
    A. Undifferentiated Faith
    B. Pre-images of God based on interaction with parents
    C. Comparable to Ericksons' trust –vs– mistrust stage of development

II. Faith Development Stages
    A. Projective Faith – Intuitive Faith (Ages 2-7)
        1. Middle childhood development (Ages 2-6)
        2. Has picture of God, Heaven, Hell
        3. Oriented towards punishment and obedience
        4. No clear personal view
            a. God's view
            b. Parent's/Guardian's view

    B. Mythical/Literal Faith (Ages 7-12)
        1. Late childhood development (Ages 6-12)
        2. Operate at a concrete level
        3. Beginning to use logic
            a. Knows difference from real and unreal
            b. Can sort through reality
        4. Moral development
        5. Has image of God
            a. Can see from God's perspective
            b. Can understand God considers intent and struggles
            c. God seen as giving good to good
            d. God seen as giving bad to bad

    C. Synthetic Conventional Faith (Adolescence and Onward)
        1. Adolescence and Young Adulthood (Ages 12-21)

---

[9] Koenig, Harold G., M.D. *Aging and God.* New York: Haworth Pastoral Press, 1993.

        2.   Can philosophize
        3.   Can conceive ideal
        4.   Need more personal relationship with God
        5.   Acceptance of belief without critical examination

D.   Individuative – Reflective Faith (Early to mid-20s or beyond)
        1.   Faith and ideology are inspected
        2.   Inspection may result from upheaval in life
            a.   Divorce
            b.   Death
            c.   Illness
            d.   Incarceration
                i.   Aging prisoner has less ability to cope
                ii.   Prison is not ideal place to cope with grief and loss (Aday)
                iii.   Kline study – took two years cope with institutionalization

E.   Conjunctive Faith – (Midlife and Beyond)
        1.   Adulthood and later life
        2.   Disillusionment with co-dependence on logic
        3.   Disillusionment with co-dependence on rational understanding
        4.   More open attitude to other faiths

F.   Universalizing Faith (Late Life)
        1.   Readiness to fellowship with persons regardless of tradition
        2.   Total commitment to a vision
        3.   Willing to give up oneself
        4.   Willing to give up life
            a.   For justice
            b.   For a transformed world to bring Kingdom of God

CONCLUSION:

"whether sudden and dramatic or gradual and stepwise, the basic change is that religious faith now becomes personally meaningful and one's relationship with God evolves to a more intimate level" (Fowler)

See chart on Religion, Aging, and Old Age.

SCRIPTURES FOR THE CYCLES OF LIFE

A. Psalm 103
B. Psalm 90
C. Psalm 116
D. Psalm 89:46-47
E. John 14:6

Meditate on these, and discuss.

FRUIT OF MATURING FAITH

A. Matthew 7:16 – By your fruit you will be recognized

B. Galatians 5:22-23 – Love, joy, peace, patience, kindness, goodness, faithfulness, gentleness, self-control

C. Ephesians 4:32 – Kind, compassionate, forgiving

D. Colossians 3:12-14 – Love, compassion, kindness, humility, gentleness, patience

E. James 3:17 – Wisdom, purity, peace-loving, considerate, submissive, mercy, good fruit, impartial, sincere

Discuss your fruit.

Questions to measure your maturity:

A. How is your fruit during success or failure?

B. How does your fruit maintain self-esteem during failure?

C. How does your fruit sustain purpose despite physical changes associated with aging?

D. You can no longer walk but you can get around in a wheel chair – describe your faith. Strong? Average? Weak?

E. You can no longer go outside – your faith?

F. You can no longer contribute to your family's well being – your faith?

G. You are in severe pain most of the time – your faith?

H. You are in severe discomfort most of the time (nausea, diarrhea) – your faith?

In light of your discussion and answers to the maturing faith questions, redo the chart for Ecclesiastes 3:1-8, note any changes.

RELIGIOSITY

A. Christian Faith
1. Behavior of prayer
2. Behavior of Bible reading
3. Meditation
4. Fellowship
5. Worship

B. Study of 1000 men at Duke University:
1. 60% religion grew in importance with aging
2. 35% importance did not change as aged
3. 5% religion grew less important as aged

RELIGION, AGING, AND OLD AGE[10]

AGE	STRONG	SOMEWHAT	NOT VERY	NO AFFILIATION	ROW TOTAL
18-29	28%	10%	48%	13%	7635
30-39	34	11	44	11	7613
40-49	39	10	42	9	5820
50-59	44	10	41	5	4576
60-69	47	11	38	4	3968
70-79	53	11	32	4	2864
80+	56	13	28	3	1128
TOTALS	13008	3507	14148	2941	33604

As one ages, there seems to be increased religiosity, as reported.

EXPLORING RELIGIOSITY'S IMPACT ON EMOTIONAL WELL-BEING IN OLD AGE[11]

Comparison of Attitude of Happiness with Health Status

	Health=Excellent		Health=Good		Health=Fair/Poor	
RELIGIOSITY:	MALES	FEMALES	MALES	FEMALES	MALES	FEMALES
Strong	63%	58%	51%	45%	30%	28%
Somewhat	61%	59%	32%	32%	30%	30%
Not Very	54%	60%	38%	32%	25%	18%
No Affiliation	45%	67%	29%	39%	18%	10%
TOTALS	58%	59%	41%	40%	27%	24%

I. James 5:7-14 – Reminders in the Lord
    A. Be patient remembering the Lord is coming

    B. (v.8) Stand firm

---

[10] Center for Aging, Religion & Spirituality, Luther Seminary, "Spirituality and The Elderly: Survey of Staff and Residents of Long-Term Care Facvilities, 1998." St. Paul, Minnesota.
[11] Ibid.

    C.   (v.10) "…in the face of suffering, take the prophets who spoke in the name of the Lord"

    D.   (v.11) "…we consider blessed those who persevered. You have heard of Job's perseverance and have seen what the Lord finally brought about. The Lord is full of compassion and mercy."

    E.   (v.13) Is anyone of you sick, call the elder…to pray… anoint… in the name of the Lord

II.   Hebrews 6:12 warns us not to give up, continue to practice faith and patience and receive God's promise

III.   Spiritual needs of aging – weights and measures
    A.   Dependence on God's grace (Aday, 309)
        1.   Isaiah 42:2 – God reminds Israel of God's grace, unmerited favor
        2.   "When you pass through the waters, I will be with you; and when you pass through the rivers, they will not sweep over you. When you walk through the fire you will not be burned, the flames will not set you ablaze." (Isaiah 43:2, NIV)

    B.   Acceptance of human limitations (Aday, 309)
        1.   Psalm 32:6
        2.   "Therefore let everyone who is godly pray to you while you may be found; surely when the mighty waters rise, they will not reach him." (Psalm 32:6, NIV)

    C.   The need to forgive past grudges and Resentments

    D.   The need to be forgiven – "Blessed is the man whose sin the Lord does not count against him." (Psalm 32:2)

    E.   The need to channel energy into rehabilitation (Aday, 293)

    F.   The need to share God's gift of loving other

G. The need to release pent-up energy

H. The need to positively face death[12]

IMPACT OF FAITH ON HEALTH AND AGING

I. Impact of faith
   A. Provides for the treatment of the elderly alcohol abuser
   B. Provides faster recovery rates
   C. Provides greater coping skills with chronic illness
   D. Provides comfort from stress
   E. Provides comfort from grief
   F. Provides comfort from pain
   G. Provides for relief of depression
   H. Provides for relief anxiety
   I. Provides comfort to the mentally impaired

II. Older adults becoming more drug (prescription) and alcohol dependent (State of Michigan Health Department).
   A. Religion enhances self-esteem
   B. Religion provides way to receive forgiveness
   C. Religion allows chronically ill with strong faith to recover faster (Koenig, 1998)

---

[12] 2 Timothy 4:7, "I have fought the good fight, I have finished the race, I have kept the faith. Now there is in store for me the crown of righteousness, which the Lord, the righteous Judge, will award to me in that day – and not only to me, but also to all who have longed for his appearing."

III. Koenig's study of 96 aging inmates:
   A. Religious belief important to adjustment and behavior

   B. Religiosity important to adjustment and behavior

   C. Religion provided structure

   D. Religion provided hope

   E. Religion provided security

   F. Religion helped inmates cope with dying

FAITH AND DYING

I. Eternal life includes physical death
   A. God's breath (Spirit) returns to Him

   B. The body returns back to dust

II. Jesus is life
   A. He is life Now

   B. He is life Future

   C. He is life Eternal

III. Facing the last season under the sun, death, requires spiritual readiness:
   A. People are living longer but death is inevitable unless the rapture is first. "We believe that Jesus died and rose again and so we believe that God will bring with Jesus those who have fallen asleep [died] in him. According to the Lord's own word, we tell you that we who are still alive, who are left till the coming of the Lord, will certainly not precede those who have fallen asleep. For the Lord himself will

come down from heaven, with a loud command, …we who are still alive and are left will be caught up together with them in the clouds to meet the Lord in the air. And so we will be with the Lord forever." (1 Thessalonians 4:14-17)

B. Be ready for the translation
   1. O.T events of no death
       a. Enoch translated without physical death
           i. Lived 365 years
           ii. By faith Enoch did not see death because God had translated him…he pleased God.
       b. The Lord sent a Chariot of Fire to translate His prophet, Elijah.
           i. Elijah went to heaven in a whirlwind
           ii. Elisha replaced him as prophet
           iii. His work was done
   2. Christ had not taken on humanity, and they went to meet Him spiritually.
       a. Matthew 17, tells us the disciples, Peter, John, and James saw Elijah and Moses with Jesus in His translated being
       b. All were transfigured – a changed appearance
       c. The body as we know it, does not get into heaven
       d. The term translated as used in KJV and translated in other versions means: as to be removed, to be changed
           i. To change
           ii. To remove
           iii. To transfer to another place
           iv. To change one's position (Vines)
   3. Being translated, a blessing for the saint
       a. Moses – with the Lord
       b. Elijah – with the Lord

            c. Paul says that death for the believer is to be with the Lord.
            d. Colossians 1:13 [God] "Who hath delivered us from the power of darkness [damnation/death], and hath translated us into the kingdom of his dear Son." (NKJV)
        4. Death
            a. Physical death – permanent cessation of all vital signs
                i. Breathing
                ii. Heart beat
                iii. Brain functions
            b. Spiritual death – antagonism with God due to unbelief in Jesus, the Christ
                i. Remain in sin
                ii. Object of God's wrath (Ephesians 2)
                iii. Second death – Lake of fire (Revelation 20:14)
                iv. No hope of redemption
                v. Separation from God (Genesis 3:22-24)
                vi. No faith in Jesus, The Christ (Romans 5:19-21)

IV. Believer accepts this physical body not in its eternal form
    A. God determines length of days
    B. David states how short is life[13]
    C. "If [God] He withdrew His Spirit, and breath, all mankind would perish together and man would return to dust" (Job 34:14-15 NIV)

V. Attitudes aiding peaceful transition
    A. Hope ever present (Psalm 33:13-22; Psalm 6:2-7))
        1. Face the future expectantly

---

[13] "Remember how fleeting is my life. For what futility you have created for all men. What man can live and not see death, or save himself from the power of the grace.

2. Know God's mercy

B. Combat 'Why Me' syndrome?
1. Recognize that innocent die (Psalm 94:21; Isaiah 59:7)
2. Recognize need to get house in order
   a. Examine past sins (Psalm 107:11
   b. Focus on God's blessings Ecclesiastes 5:16-20)
   c. Accept God's will (Ecclesiastes 7:13-14)
   d. Accept God's control (Job 42:2-3)

3. Decide what (if any) life supports you wish
   a. Know what medical procedures you wish to prolong life
   b. Know that God still performs miracles

C. Scriptures to Read:
1. Ecclesiastes 7:13-14 "Consider what God has done…when times are good, be happy; but when times are bad, consider: God has made the one as well as the other." (NIV)
2. Job 42:2-3, "I know that You can do all things; no plan of yours can be thwarted. You asked, 'Who is this that obscures my counsel without knowledge?' Surely I spoke of things I did not understand, things too wonderful for me to know." (NIV)
3. Remember Psalm 139:16, " All the days ordained for me were written in your book before one of them came to be
4. The time will come for Psalm 142:7, "Set me free from my prison, that I may praise your name. Then the righteous will gather about me because of your goodness to me." (NIV)

NEW LIFE

I. Life gets better – 1 Corinthian 15:38
    A. God gives…a body as He has determined

    B. 15:42 …with the resurrection of the dead
        1. The body that is sown is perishable,
        2. Raised imperishable
        3. Sown in dishonor
        4. Raised in glory
        5. Sown in weakness
        6. Raised in power
        7. Sown a natural body
        8. Raised a Spiritual body

    C. 15:44 "If there is a natural body, there is also a spiritual body" (NIV)

    D. 15:49 "Just as we have born the likeness of the earthly man, so shall we bear the likeness of the man from heaven" (NIV)

II. Flesh and blood cannot inherit the kingdom of God, nor does the perishable inherit the imperishable…we will all be changed
    A. Death has been swallowed in victory

    B. Death where is your victory?

    C. Death where is your sting?

    D. Thanks be to God! He gives us the victory through our Lord Jesus Christ. (15:50, 57)

BIBLIOGRAPHY AND SUGGESTED BOOKS

Aday, Ronald H. *Aging Prisoners.* Westport, CT. Praeger Publishing, 2003.

Barron, Robert, Brubaker, J. Omar, and Clark, Robert E. *Understanding People.* Evangelistic Training Association, 1985.

Clements, R.E., "Wisdom and Health", *Wisdom in Theology.* Erdsman, (1992): 65-93.

Crabb, Lawrence, Ph.D. *Understanding People.* Grand Rapids. MI: Zondervan, 1987.

Johnson, Eric L., and Jones, Stanton L. Eds. *Psychology and Christianity.* Downers Grove, IL: Intervarsity Press, 2000.

Harris, R. Laird, Archer, Jr, Gleason L. and Waltke, Bruce K. *Theological Wordbook of the Old Testament, Volumes 1 &2.* Chicago, IL: Moody Press, 1980.

Koenig, Harold G., M.D. *Aging and God.* New York: Haworth Pastoral Press, 1993.

Koenig, Harold G, M.D. and Weaver, Andrew J. *Pastoral Care of Older Adults.* Minneapolis, MN: Fortress, 1998.

Riekse, Robert & Holstege, Henry. *Growing Older in America.* New York: McGraw Hill, 1996.

Vines, W.E., Unger, Merrill F., White, Jrl, Williams, *Vine's Complete Expository Dictionary of Old and New Testament Words.* Nashville, TN: Thomas Nelson Publishers, 1985.

Zucker, Robert A., et al, *Fundamentals of Alcohol and Other Drug Problems.* Michigan Department of Community Health Center for Substance Abuse. 1996.

BIBLES

_____.*The Amplified Bible.* Grand Rapids, MI: Zondervan, 1987.

Barker, Kenneth. Gen. Ed. *The NIV Study Bible New International Version.* Grand Rapids, MI: Zondervan, 1985.

Scofield, C.I. D.D., Ed. *The New Scofield Study Bible, New King James Version.* Nashville, TN: Thomas Nelson Publishers, 1989.

Chapter 2
THE DIE IS CAST

Decision Making in the Will of God

BSJ Christian Seminars
Minister Brenda Simuel Jackson, Ph.D.
© 2004 All rights reserved.

This sign at the prison in Pretoria, South Africa reads:
NOTICE: ENTERING PREMISES AT OWN RISK!

SEMINAR OBJECTIVES

- Learn the difference between God's sovereign and Moral Wills and individual life plans
- Know the relationship of making choices and derived decision-making
- Use wisdom in decision-making
- Know how to evaluate your decisions
- Know the results of effective decisions made

DECISIONS
© Brenda Simuel Jackson

A decision, the conclusion of the matter, beginning anew.
A decision, making choices in our lives where the choice right or wrong may stick to us like glue.

A decision, following guidelines from above will guide us through dangers and toils with cords of love.

Decisions that follow our lust, fleshy desires, and a moment of thrill are the ones that result in choices that kill.

Some decisions are not ours to make, but their results are ours to leave or take.

Some decisions affect us for a life time; there is one decision that is not bound by this life's span or time but must be made while the body lives, to receive the gift that is not ours to give.

The Preacher said there is a time for everything; there is no real time for wrong decisions; the time is always right for decisions that follow God's will and His might.

DECISION MAKING

I. A Decision:
    A.   A determination
    B.   A conclusion to a matter

II. Critical life decisions made
    A.   The disciples – Matthew 4:18-22
        1. Simon and Andrew made life decisions
        2. Jesus called Simon (Peter) and His brother Andrew (fishermen)
            i. Follow Me, I will make you fishers of men
            ii. They left their nets and followed
            iii. They left the old way of life to follow a new life
            iv. Made choice for the Kingdom of Heaven
        3. Jesus called James and his brother John, who were preparing nets
            i. They left the boat
            ii. They left their father
            iii. They followed
            iv. They made a choice, a decision
    B.   Decisions made by disciples were in line with God's Perfect Will.
    C.   Decisions made were in line with God's Sovereign Will.
    D.   Decisions made were in line with God's Moral Will.
    E.   Decisions of disciples in line with God's Prevailing Will.[14]
    F.   Decisions of disciples part of God's Permissive Will
        1. Each disciple made a choice
        2. Each disciple could have said no

---

[14] Proverbs 19:21, "Many are the plans in a man's heart, but it is the Lord's purpose that prevails.) (NIV)

III. Decision Making
    A. "Making a decision is a process that includes making a choice, make judgments": (Friesen)
        1. Thoughts
        2. Attitudes
        3. Actions
    B. Decisions, an act of our will, subject to influence:
        1. Our desires (flesh)
        2. Our mind
        3. Our emotions
        4. The guidance of The Holy Spirit

BIBLICAL HISTORICAL DECISION MAKING

I. Urim and Thummin[15]
    A. Determiners of God's Will
        1. On golden breastplate inside were two lots
        2. Lots placed over heart of Aaron whenever he entered the presence of the Lord.

    B. Lot is a die which is colored black on one side, white on other
        1. Two white meant yes
        2. Two black meant no
        3. Black and white meant wait

    C. Exodus 28:30 "...Thus Aaron will always bear the means of making decisions for the Israelites over his heart before the Lord." (NIV)
        1. Know – The heart is place of reasoning and emotions
        2. Before The Lord – decision-making
            a. Consulting the Lord
            b. Being advised by the Lord
            c. Being in the presence of The Lord

---

[15] Lawrence Richards, Ph.D. *The Revell Bible Dictionary*. Grand Rapids, MI: Fleming H. Revell Co., 1990, 1002.

        d. Numbers 27:21 "He will stand before Eleazar, the Priest, who will obtain decisions for him by inquiring of the Urim before the Lord…" (NASB)

II. Decisions based on revelation
    A. Casting lots (Proverbs 18:18)
        1. Settles disputes
        2. Keeps strong opponents apart
    B. The land, a lot, determined by casting lots
    C. The lot is used by God
        1. Proverb 16:33, "The lot is cast into the lap, but its every decision is from the Lord." (NIV)
        2. Is it chance
        3. God controls chance

III. Decisions based on a sign
    A. The fleece method (Judges 6:36-40)
        1. Gideon made a decision based on a sign requested from the Lord
        2. Gideon wanted to ensure his action would be of the Lord

    B. Group – We put out fleeces to test our decisions?
        1. Are we seeking revelation?
        2. Are we seeking a sign?
        3. Are we using wisdom?
        4. Are we seeking self justification for a decision made?

    C. A gamble
        1. Decisions should not be a gamble
        2. In time of Christ, gamblers were not allowed to give evidence in court (Gower, 2005)
            a. Gamblers not trusted
            b. Game of Baseleus (Greek for King)
                i. Move wooden skittle on ground according to throw of dice.

  ii. Game included robbing, crowning, and scepter
  iii. Soldiers used Jesus for the game:
- Crowned with thorns
- Robbed Him
- Gave Him a scepter
- The person crowned was the winner

IV. The perfect decision:
 A. Making decisions according to God's Will
  1. Key to Spiritual success in decisions made (Friesen, p.30)
   a. Must know God's Will
   b. Must obey His Will
  2. Two key questions: (Group Discussion)
   a. Does God have an individual plan for each believer?
   b. Is there freedom of choice among plans?

 B. God's Will
  1. Revealed expectation for human moral behavior
  2. God is sovereign
  3. God is in control (Friesen, p. 30)
   a. God's predetermined plan for all things is the Master plan
   b. God's sovereign will does not exclude need for planning
   c. God's sovereign will requires an attitude of humility and submissiveness
  4. Job 42:2: "I know that you can do all things."
   a. No plan of yours can be thwarted
   b. We pray God's will, not ours, be done (Matthew 6:10)

 C. God determines if our decision will be put into effect (James 4:14-15 NIV)

1. "…you do not even know what will happen tomorrow."
2. What is your life? You are mist…then vanishes
3. "Instead you ought to say, if it is the Lord's will, we will live and do this or that."
4. Submissive attitude toward decisions made

D. God's will is divine

E. Jesus submissive to God's will (Matthew 26:42, "My Father, if it is not possible for this cup to be taken away unless I drink it, may your will be done.") NIV

F. Individual plans (Richards, 2004)
 1. God's will include His plan for the individual
 2. God knows what will happen
 3. God does not tell us all things
 4. It is not our plan
 5. It is how God uses us in His plan for His purpose[16]
 6. Jeremiah 29:11, "For I know the thoughts and plans I have for you, says the Lord, thoughts and plans for welfare and peace, and not for evil, to give you hope in your final outcome." (AMP)

G. God's Plan/Purpose
 1. Israel was told to put themselves under the yoke of Babylon – punishment for 70 years.
 2. Jeremiah told them to prepare:
    a. Marry
    b. Have children
    c. The Lord will redeem in 70 years
    d. The Lord will return them to the land
 3. The False prophet seeking to effect the decision:
    a. The Lord will break the yoke in two years

---

[16] Ephesians 1:11 (Amplified): In Him we also were made [God's] heritage (portion) and we obtained an inheritance; for we had been foreordained (chosen and appointed beforehand) in accordance with His purpose, Who works out everything in agreement with the counsel and design of His [own] will.

       b. False prophet died less than a year later for lying against The Lord.
       c. Must know God's will
       d. Know God's will includes punishment in the plan
    4. We have hope for the future

H. God's plan for the individual:
    1. Revealed expectation for moral behavior
    2. Resist personal will

I. God's perfect will (Romans 12:2; 1 Corinthians 13:10-12)[17]
    1. Perfect is completion
       a. Maturity
       b. Finished
       c. Complete
    2. Complete revelation of God's will and way
    3. Renew the mind to know the will of God
       a. Discernment of the believer
       b. Guided by the Holy Spirit

J. Moral Will of God:
    1. Be holy for I am holy (1 Peter 1:16; Leviticus 11:44-45)
    2. Decisions should have Character of God
       a. Morally right
       b. Peaceful
       c. Powerful
       d. Provisional
       e. Other directed
    3. Proper attitude – knowing God is in control

---

[17] "But when perfection comes, the imperfect disappears. When I was a child, I talked like a child, I thought like a child, I reasoned like a child. When I became a man, I put childish ways behind me." (NIV)

Choice and Decision-Making

I. Choices Requiring Knowledge of God's Will:

Scripture	Decisions?	Do I Need to Know God's Will – Yes	Do I Need to Know God's Will - No
Genesis 2:18 Corinthians 7:8-9	Shall I marry? Whom Shall I marry?		
2 Timothy 2:15-16 Proverbs 6:10-11	Should I go to college? What car should I buy?		

    A.   Discuss and add to the Scriptures before making any decisions

    B.   Add to the list of decisions needed, and search the scriptures for the will of God.

II. Man created with ability to make decisions:
    A.   Adam named the animals – given freedom to make choices (Genesis 2:19,20)

    B.   Garden of Eden
        1. Man told he had choice to select from any tree
        2. Denied the choice of tree of knowledge of good and evil
            a. Area of freedom of choice
            b. Freedom to obey/disobey

    C.   David's punishment (1 Chronicles 21:10)
        1. The Lord gave David three options
        2. David had choice of punishment – limited by options

    D.   Convinced of right choices, right decisions: (Romans 14:5,10,12)
        1. Let each person be fully convinced in own mind
        2. We will stand before judgment of God
        3. We will give an account to God for our choices

REVELATIONS
(Knowledge of Hidden Truths Aids Decision Making)

Types and Sources of Revelation

GENERAL REVELATION	SPECIFIC REVELATION
God disclosing Himself to all persons in all places (Psalm 19:1-6)	God disclosing Himself to specific persons by supernatural and specific modes.

General:

Type	What	Scriptures
Revelation through nature	God's omnipotence	Romans 1:18-21
	God's judgments	Romans 1:18-21
	God's glory	Psalm 19:1-6
	God's existence	Psalm 19:1-6
	God's supremacy	Romans 1:20
Revelation through God's provisions (blessings)	The sun and the rain	Mathew 5:45
	The heaven, the earth, the sea	Acts 14:15
	Food, joy	Acts 14:17
	Seasons, ages, wisdom, knowledge	Daniel 2:21
Revelation through Consciousness	What is right and wrong; man's moral nature	Romans 2:14-15
Revelation from a sense of a higher being	Worshipping in ignorance (the unknown God)	Acts 17:22-31
Revelation through condemnation	God's wrath against ungodliness	Romans 1:18-19

God ensures that all have a sense that He is!

Specific:

Revelation through specific persons by special means – Scriptures	Revelation through history	Revelation through Christ	Revelation through the Holy Spirit
The casting of lots communicates God's intent (Acts 1:21-26; Proverbs 16:33)	To certain peoples through events in history: Micah 6:4-5-Egypt and Balaam; Exodus 14 – The Red Sea	The Incarnation of the Word (John 3:16; Hebrews 1:1-3)	Expresses the very thoughts of God (1 Corinthians 2:1-16; Romans 8:16)
The Urim & Thummin communicated God's decision (Exodus 28:30 [judgments], Numbers 27:21; 1 Samuel 28:6)		His testimony of the Word. (Matthew 5:17-19)	Teachings of the Holy Spirit. (1 Corinthians 2:6-16)
Through dreams (Genesis 20:3,6, 11-13)		His testimony of the inerrancy of scripture (John 10:35)	Reveals the truth of Jesus Christ (John 15:26-27)
Through vision (Isaiah 1:1; 6:1; Ezekiel 1:1-3)		The words of Jesus Christ (John 12:49)	
Theophanies, Angel of the Lord [Christ] (Genesis 16:7-14 [Hagar])		The fulfillment of the law and the prophets (Luke 24:44)	
Through angels (Luke 2:9-11)			
Through prophets (Ephesians 3:5-9, Zechariah 1:1,2; 2 Samuel 22:2)			
Scriptures testimony of Christ (John 5:46)			

Note: Salvation is a specific revelation through Christ.

Questions on general revelation:
What decisions do we make that are impacted by general revelation?
- Travel
- Purchases
- God's Supremacy

Questions of specific revelation:
What decision do we make that impacted by specific revelation?
- What happened in history that guides today's decision?
- What did Christ say that had an impact?
- What did the Holy Spirit teach?

WISDOM AND DECISION MAKING
(James 1:2-8; 3:13-18; 1 Corinthians 1:18-3:23)

I. One's life style is evidence of having or lacking true wisdom.
   A. True wisdom comes with true faith.
   B. Trials of life: (James 1:2-5)
      1. Inevitable
      2. Being in jail for cause – not a trial
      3. Being in jail for cause – judgment/justice
      4. Trails encountered while being in judgment:
         a. Losing family
         b. Losing material possessions
         c. Illness
         d. Paul's trials while incarcerated:
            i. Ship wrecked
            ii. Snake bite
      5. Benefit to a trial
         a. Endurance
         b. Maturity
         c. Spiritual fulfillment
         d. Becoming what God wants us to

II. Lacking wisdom – unable to endure trials

A. Wisdom – to teach

B. Different aspects of term wisdom:
   1. Hebrew Term – used for understanding
   2. Hebrew Term – used for intelligence
   3. Psalm 39:26 "Does the hawk take flight by your wisdom and spread his wings toward the south?" (NIV)
      a. Who created the hawk?
      b. Whose wisdom is operating?
   4. Wisdom – a skill (talent)
      a. Exodus 28:3, "Tell all the skilled men to whom I have given wisdom in such matters that they are to make garments…" (NIV)
      b. Ecclesiastes 1:13 " I devoted myself to study and to explore by wisdom all that is done under heaven." (NIV)
   5. Wisdom – Using discretion (Daniel 2:14: "Daniel spoke with wisdom and tact." NIV)
   6. Wisdom is heart

III. Trials lead to maturity:
   A. Maturity reached – A goal
   B. Maturity process of growth
   C. Maturity a sign of wisdom

IV. Wisdom is a life style (James 3:13-18)
   A. Results of man's wisdom
      1. Envy
      2. Selfish ambition
      3. Disorder
      4. Evil practices

   B. Results of man's wisdom from God
      1. Godly life style
      2. Pure
      3. Peace-loving
      4. Considerate
      5. Submissive
      6. Mercy

7. Good fruit
8. Impartial
9. Sincere

V. N.T Greek term for wisdom is Sophia (1 Corinthians 1:18 – 3:23)
   A. Wisdom is truth

   B. Real nature of things

   C. Wisdom
      1. Human wisdom
         a. Man's wisdom futile compared to power and wisdom of God
         b. Man's brilliance cannot appreciate plan of God's salvation (1 Corinthians 1:18-21)
         c. Man's knowledge not know what needs
         d. Only depend on God for true knowledge of needs (Knowledge p.509)
      2. Practical wisdom
         a. Unusual ability
         b. Skill
         c. Knowledge of God's will
         d. Insight to apply God's will to our daily lives
      3. Spiritual wisdom (foolish)
         a. Know that one cannot apply human wisdom to spiritual matters
         b. Worldly wisdom did not bring man to knowledge of God (1 Corinthians 1:18-31)
            i. Jews demanded miracles
            ii. Greeks philosophical system
         c. Human wisdom may leave Christ out (1 Corinthians 1:24-30)
         d. Gain spiritual wisdom through teachings of the Holy Spirit
         e. Search the Scriptures:
            i. 1 Corinthians 2:13-16
            ii. 2 Timothy 3:15
            iii. 2 Peter 3:15
            iv. Only Spiritual people receive spiritual messages (wisdom – 1 Corinthians 2:14)

4. God's Wisdom
   a. Plan of Salvation (Matthew 11:24-26)
   b. Creation
   c. Christ alone personifies wisdom from God (vv 1 Corinthians 29-31)
   d. Faith not a product of knowledge, but of God's spiritual revelation
      i. Faith results in stability in Jesus Christ
      ii. Faith results in knowing His wisdom will sustain
      iii. Faith gives wisdom to lean on Him (Proverb 3:5)

D. How to get wisdom
   1. James says ask, don't doubt
   2. Proverbs 2:6,9-10,12
      a. The Lord gives wisdom
      b. His word is wisdom
      c. Wisdom in the heart
      d. Wisdom from knowledge

E. Exhibiting wisdom:
   1. Practical living
   2. Relationship with God
   3. Our approach to life
   4. Guided by God's Will in making choices
   5. Applying divine guidelines to every day situations
   6. Subjecting self to God
   7. Sensitive to God

Summary:
"Wisdom – practical combines knowledge and experience to successfully meet moral or other challenges in daily life which exhibits wisdom." (NIV Encyclopedia)

Thank God for the opportunity to select from acceptable alternatives (Friesen).
- Choose personal preferences
- Apply maturity by gathering data
- Devote sufficient time to the process

- Put personal desires in proper perspective
- Use sound reason

Know the area specifically addressed as revealed by the Bible:
- The moral will requires obedience
- Commands require obedience
- Areas where Bible gives no clear command or principle (non-moral) use wisdom to chart the course

A decision process:
- Determine the purpose of the decision
- Determine if there are spiritual goals which require divine revelation
- Determine the importance (priority) of the decision
- Submit decision to prayer for God's sovereign will (Pray according to God's will)
- Did the decision pass the morality test?
- Will the decision glorify God?
- Know the leading of the Holy Spirit (John 16:12-14)
- Develop strategies to achieve decision(s) made

EXAMINE YOUR DECISIONS

- Family contact?
- Living arrangements?
- Education?
- Employment goals?
- Mentor?
- Church?
- Friends?

Add your own items, based on your current life style.

References and Suggested Readings

_____, *Amplified Bible Version.* Grand Rapids, MI: Zondervan, 1987.

Barker, Kenneth, Gen. Ed. *The NIV Study Bible, New International Version.* Grand Rapids, MI: Zondervan, 1985.

Friesen, Garry and Maxson, J. Robin. *Decision Making and The Will of God.* Portland, OR: Multnomah, 1980.

Gower, Ralph. *The New Manners and Customs of Bible Times.* Chicago, IL: Moody Press, 2005.

Hunt, June. *Counseling Through The Bible.* Dallas TX: Hope For The Heart, 2004.

Richards, Ph.D. Lawrence O. *The Revell Bible Dictionary.* New Jersey: Fleming H. Revell Co., 1990.

Richards, Lawrence O. *New International Encyclopedia of Bible Words, Based on the NIV and the NASB.* Grand Rapids, MI: Zondervan Publishing House, 2004.

Vine, W.E. Unger, Merrill F., and White, William. *Vines Complete Expository Dictionary Of Old and New Testament Words.* Nashville, TN: Nelson Publishers, 1985.

Walvoord, John F. and Zuck, Roy B. Ed. *The Bible Knowledge Commentary.* Colorado Springs, CO: Chariot Victor Publishing, 1997.

Chapter 3
SELECTING THE EASY YOKE

Breaking Yokes

BSJ Christian Seminars
Minister Brenda Simuel Jackson, Ph.D.
© 2005 All rights reserved.

Transcending Transformation

© Brenda Simuel Jackson

Dedicated to the Women of Huron Valley Correctional Complex

Out for the count, when I received my sentence.
Out from my known world to a place of unknown qualities.
Worldly clothes taken, and prison garb received,
a fashion plate of difference? Please!

The Chaplain provided opportunities for me to see my past world,
and to start my life over, if only my soul would unfurl.
In the world, I conformed to what was for my convenience,
but now conformance is because I am doing penitence.

The volunteers, invited by the Chaplain,
open the way for true change
to transform myself into a new creation,
to stand above all my worldly sensations.

Freedom through Jesus Christ; He broke all my chains,
and now daily living is with the Holy Spirit, Who truly holds the reins.
My spiritual gifts are becoming evident,
and my talents are constantly showing my confidence.

Like the caterpillar, I am transformed, and like the eagle,
I transcend to higher heights of God's love and His Word.
Down for the count, not I, there are many rounds in
my transformation which will forever transcend my past life of sin.

There are no rules against soaring in Christ!
My transformed life is so nice.

SEMINAR OBJECTIVES

- Identify what are the various types of yokes.
    - Yokes that burden
    - Yokes that set free
- Identify means of breaking physical yokes through living in self-control of the Spirit.
- Establish goals to remain free from yokes that burden

FOUNDATIONAL SCRIPTURES

- Matthew 11:28-29 (Amplified Version)

Come to Me, all you who labor and are heavy laden and *overburdened*, and I will cause you to rest. [I will ease and relieve and refresh your souls.] Take my yoke upon you and learn of Me, for I am gentle (meek) and humble (lowly) in heart, and you will find (relief and ease and refreshment and recreation and blessed quiet for your souls. [Jeremiah 6:16]

- Matthew 11:30 (Amplified Version)

For My yoke is Wholesome (useful, good – not harsh, hard, sharp or pressing, but comfortable, gracious, and pleasant), and My burden is light and easy to be borne.

- Galatians 5:1 (Amplified Version)

In [this] freedom Christ has made us free [and completely liberated us]; stand fast then, and do not be hampered and held ensnared and submit again to a yoke of slavery [which you have once put off].

- Galatians 5:25 (Amplified Version)

If we live by the [Holy] Spirit, let us also walk by the Spirit. [If by the Holy Spirit we have our life in God, let us go forward walking in line, our conduct controlled by the Spirit.

What is a Yoke?

- Generic – Denotative
    - Wooden bar to join two at the head or neck to enable working together
    - A device laid on the neck of a defeated person.
    - A device fitted to a person's shoulder t carry a heavy burden
    - An oppressive agency
        - Servitude
        - Bondage
        - Tie
        - Link
- Biblical Overview
    - Old Testament – imposed on the neck
        - A pole
        - A Band
        - Isaiah 10:27: A burden to be broken by the strong and sturdy.
        - As Israel grew strong, broke the hold of millions.
        - 1 Kings 12:4: Heavy labor without consent, forced labor.
        - Labor of Israelites under Solomon and Rehoboam.
    - New Testament – Greek term means to join
        - Verb
            - To put to work
            - To be linked
            - To be obligated

Sampling of Yokes of Destructive Habits

- Yokes which burden a person, physically, Spiritually, Mentally
    - Cheating
    - Compulsive gambling
    - Gossip/Slander
    - Immorality
    - Lying
    - Pornography
    - Profanity
    - Sexual perversion
    - Rage
    - Sexual addiction
    - Stealing
    - Substance Abuse
    - Violence
    - Worry
    - Yokes that Oppress
        - Lamentation 1:14
        - Sins will press down and sap your strength
    - Yokes of Unnatural service
        - Leviticus 26:13
        - Yoke of involuntary slaves, being bowed down as was Israel under Egypt.
- Positive Yokes
    - Yoke of submission to Spiritual Authority

- Matthew 11:29,30
- Galatians 5:1

FOUR YOKES OF ABOMINATION
(Yokes learning to break in this Seminar)

- Lying
- Stealing
- Excessive Drinking
- Worrying

THE HABITUAL LIAR: The Deceiver
- To Beguile[18] – Old Testament meaning
  - Deal treacherously
  - In Aramaic, be sluggish
    - Be putrid
    - Be corrupt
  - Deceive
  - Mislead
- The Craft of Deception – Old Testament Meaning:
  - To deceive as a craft such as fraud.
  - Deceit of balances is called craftiness.
- Another root term is translated as lying means to cheat.
  - To e untrue
- The Falsehood
  - Opposite of falsehood is <u>faithfulness:</u>
    - Falsehood – inability to keep faith

---

[18] When used to mean deceit or treachery, often refers to spoken speech.

- Vain words (Exodus 5:9) are lies
- Deceptive speech

  - Greek pseudo meaning fictitious[19]
    - Describes hypocritical liars
    - Deceptive spirits (demons)
  - Idolatry
    - A lie – an idol worshipped in lieu of God (Romans 1:25)
    - The lie, a man made idol (Isaiah 44:20)
  - Pathological Lying ("Counseling Through The Bible, June Hunt, p. 3)
    - Compulsive Lying
    - Vague
    - Seemingly Purposeless
    - May believe the Lies
    - May have no discernible guilt

---

[19] English tern is pseudonymn.

IN THE BEGINNING THERE WAS DECEPTION

Scriptures	Deceit	Context	Outcome/injuries
Genesis 3:1-4	Satan deceives Eve	Satan seeking to displace God	Fall of man, beginning of original sin.
Genesis 20:1-4	Abraham deceives Abimelech saying Sarah is his sister[20]	Abraham seeks to protect himself from one with ore power[21]	Abimelech took Sarah and The Lord was on the verge of destroying a nation.
Genesis 27:5	Rebekah and Jacob deceive Isaac	Isaach believes he is dying and as custom, he is giving the blessing to the eldest son which is not Jacob.	Jacob gets Isaac's blessing, and then must flee to avoid the wrath of Esau, the family is split. Sarah never saw her son again.
Genesis 29:15-27	Leban deceives Jacob giving him Leah as wife and not his love.	Jacob Hs requested Rebekah, worked seven years for her dowry to have her as wife, but she was the youngest, and Leah the oldest.	Beginning of a rif between Jacob and Leban, and Jacob had two wives, and not only the one he truly loved.
Genesis 39:7-21	Joseph is imprisoned because he refused the advances of Potiphar's wife.	The wife was pursuing Joseph a servant and he refused to violate his master's trust, and she lied against him, and accused him of molesting her.	Joseph, innocent, imprisoned for two years

---

[20] Sarah is Abraham's half sister.
[21] Abraham lied twice to gain personal protection, showing a lack of trust in God, and putting his wife at risk.

MY PERSONAL EXAMINATION

My Deception	The Context	The Outcome

GOD'S COMMANDS

Colossians 3:9-10

- Do not lie to each other since you have taken off your old self with its practices, and have put on the new self, which is being renewed in knowledge in the image of its creator.
- Ephesians 4:25

Therefore each of you must put off falsehood and speak truthfully to his neighbor, for we are all lmembers of one body.

Anatomy of the Falsehood

- F – Fallacies against The Logos, Poor Logic
- A- Anti-Christ, going ainst the truth of God
- L – Lies accepted in lieu of the Truth of God
- S – Self-centered, and not Christ-centered
- E – Evilness over righteousness
- H – Honor of thievery
- O – Odor of deception
- O – Oneness with demons
- D – Deceit is your god (Idol)
- Richards says: "There is a call to live with each other honestly sharing realities rather than attempting to project illusions that made us appear better than we are. The portrait of falsehood and deceit suggested by the Hebraic word is far from pretty. Actions are words designed to deceive are not supported by reality, worse they violate the basic relationships of trust and honesty that are to exist between human beings."

Breaking the Yoke of Lying and Putting on the Yoke of Truth

- Know you are not accountable for how others respond to the truth (1 timothy 2:25-26)
- Know the consequences of deceit. (Psalm 5:6)
- Examine Your motives (Psalm 51:6)
- Determine to be honest with God. (Psalm 32)
- Depend on the Strength of Christ to enable your change. (Philippians 4:13)
- Know God's Word about lying and deceitfulness.
- Pray
    - Discern truth from lies
    - Conviction in all deceit
    - Know the full consequences of any manner of deceit.
    - Boldness to speak truth factually, and with love.
- Treat Truth as a Valued Treasure (Counseling through The Bible, Ibid)
    - Consciously choose truth over a lie
    - Check your life style to see how it measures sto God's truth scale
    - Always report the full truth with all facts
    - Reverence Truth
    - Ask Yourself:
        - Did I speak truth?   Did I act truthfully?
        - Did I Omit truth?   Were my motives righteous?

PERSONAL INVENTORY

Identify and examine lies told/telling although did not think of them as lies initially. Journal the results.

____   I have no money.

____   I have a conflict and I cannot attend.

____   I feel good.

____   I quit smoking without a struggle.

____   I don't steal.

____   I always seek the good of the other person.

____   I always seek the truth.

II. STEALING
God's Commands Regarding "Stealing":
- Exodus 20:15 – You shall not steal
- Leviticus 19:11 – "…I am the Lord your God. Do not steal, do not lie. Do not deceive one another. Do not swear falsely by my name, and so profane the name of your God…Do not defraud your neighbor or rob him. Do not hold back the wages of a hired man overnight.
- Matthew 19:18: "… do not steal…

Anatomy of Stealing
- Act of stealing is same as lying.
    - As an adjective: Act of cover-up
        - 2 Samuel 19:3, The men **stole** into the city that day as men **steal** in who are ashamed when they flee from battle
        - Cowards
    - As verb: To steal by implication is to deceive.
    - As a righteous motive:

- Proverbs 6:30-31- "Men do not despise a thief if he steals to satisfy his hunger when he is *starving*. Yet if he is *caught, he must pay sevenfold*, though it cost him all the wealth of his house."
  - Legal Fraud, Luke 19:8:
    - In the collection of taxes fraudulently [with government sanction], overcharging.
    - "Zacchaeus as chief publican admitted possible fraud, but agreed to restore fourfold, if found. (Customs and Manners, p. 178.)

Denotative Meaning of Stealing (Webster)
- Taking without right of permission that which belongs to another.
- Keeping others from receiving what is their right.
- Synonyms for stealing (New World Thesaurus)
  - Filch
  - Loot
  - Rob
  - Purloin
  - Embezzle
  - Defraud
  - Appropriate
  - Abduct
  - Strip
  - Poach
  - Swindle
  - Plagiarize
  - Blackmail

- Shoplift
- Fleece
- Plunder
- Slander
- Extort
- Kleptomania[22] (Webster's Dictionary)
- Copyright infringement

---

[22] Persistent neurotic impulse to steal, without economic motive, only an emotional reward,.

Self Examination of Personal Theft

Stealing from God:
- I did not pay tithes and offering.
- I did not serve God with my talents.
- I have not served God with my time.

Stealing from an Office:
- I used supplies for personal use.
- I took a friend to lunch and charged it to business.
- I charged personal items to the company.
- I used company gas for personal use.
- I used the copier without paying for personal copies.
- I cam to work late, and/or left early.
- I called in sick when I was not sick.

Stealing from Businesses:
- I kept an overpayment.
- I falsified insurance claims.
- I violated copyright laws.
- Idownloaded someone else's music without paying.

Stealing from relatives, Friends, Strangers:
- I have taken money.
- I Have borrowed items, and failed to return them.
- I have received monies fraudulently.

- I cheat at play.
- O live at home without paying rent or purchasing food, or paying toward utilities.
- I have stolen items, sold, or pawned them.
- I have found items with identification and failed to return them.

Stealing from Government:
- I claimed invalid deductions on my income taxes.
- I purchased personal items with a tax exempt number.
- I claimed charitable contributions not made.
- I did not pay duty on all items purchased outside of the country.

Others form of stealing:
- I collected rent from property I did not own.
- I fraudulently hooked into someone else's utility(ies).
- I used someone else's identify to obtain credit, monies, service.

BREAKING THE YOKE OF STEALING

- Pray and ask God to re4veal to you the ways in which you steal, and have stolen.
- Confess the results to a person who will hold you accountable.
- Start a journal, and record all things stolen, and actions taken for restoration.
- Pray for God to reveal to you any false rationalizations (i.e. he.she owes me).
- Listen to the prompting of the Holy Spirit.
- Put on the Full Armor (Ephesians 6:13-18)
- Seek and accept forgiveness from God.
- Seek forgiveness of those sinned against.
- Seek to make restitution.
- Remember stealing is disobedience to God.
- Remember stealing dishonors God. (Proverbs 30:9b)
- Tell yourself:
    - Stealing says I do not trust God. (Matthew 7:25-32)
    - Stealing puts priority on possessions for fulfillment.
    - Stealing says I am smarter than anyone else.
    - Stealing is a way of vengeance, God said vengeance is His.
- Avoid being jealous.
- Avoid Envying.
- Remember Ephesians 4:28:
    - He who has been stealing must steal no longer, but must work doing something useful with his own hands, that he may have something to share with those in need.
    - Seek to help not to harm.

Remember Philippians 4:19: "My God will meet all your needs according to his glorious riches in Christ Jesus.

ALCOHOL ABUSE and GETTING HIGH
(Being drunk on fermented drink)

1 Thessalonians 5:6-11:
So then, let us not be like others, who are asleep, but let us be alert and self-controlled. For those who sleep, sleep at night, and those who get drunk, get drunk at night. But since we belong to the day, let us be self-controlled, putting on faith and love as a breastplate, and the hope of salvation as a helmet. For God did not appoint us to suffer wrath but to receive salvation through our Lord Jesus Christ. He died for us so that, whether we are awake or asleep, we may live together with Him. Therefore encourage one another and build each other up, just as in fact you are doing.

- It is getting drunk that puts us in darkness.
- Addiction:
    - Compulsive use of substances
        - Drugs (includes prescriptions)
        - Alcohol
        - Chocolate or other edibles
        - Carbonated drinks such as colas

Compulsive Drinking:

Biblical History – Strong Drink – Two types of Wine
- Unfermented wine (New Wine) associated with blessings
- Fermented Drink:
    - Feasts
    - Gifts
    - Special occasions
- Initially wine, beer, acceptable social drink.
- Fermentation, chemical change.
- The Last Supper:
    - Phase is "fruit of the Vine", Matthew 26:29. (NIV, NASB, The Greek New Testament)
        - May be fermented
        - May be unfermented

Drinking that is not of the Spirit:

Drink	Drunkenness
Ecclesiastes 10:17: Persons are blessed who drink not to get drunk.	Ephesians 5:18: Do not get drunk on wine, leads to debauchery (Greek term for orgies, wantonness, licentiousness.)
Deuteronomy 7:13: Unfermented wine is associated with a blessing as in produce/crop.	1 Corinthian 5:11: Do not associate with a Christian (brother or sister) who is a drunkard.
1 Samuel 25:18: Fermented wine given as a gift of reconciliation and sustenance.	Galatians 5:19,21: The acts of the sinful nature...envy, drunkenness, orgies.
Numbers 6:3: Strong drink is any fermented fruit or grain.	1 Corinthian 11:19-22: Getting drunk is humiliating and raising the question of despising the Church of God.
Diluted wine used in Passover (Customs and d Manners)	Proverbs 20:1: Drunkenness shows lack of wisdom.
Exodus 29:40: Drink Offering sacrificed to God has a pleasant aroma.	Proverbs 21:17b: lavish drinking will cause the loss of riches
Genesis 14:18: Drink is used for refreshment.	Habakkkuk 2:15: Drunkenness leads to immoral behavior, and anyone who causes such drinking will be judged.
2 Chronicle 11:11: Wine used in time of war to give soldiers strength in case of a siege.	2 Samuel 13:28: Will cause one not to be aware of the danger around them.
Deuteronomy 14:26: Wine or other fermented drink used to rejoice before the Lord.	Proverbs 31:4: Persons in authority are not to crave strong drink because their drinking may cause them to forget laws, and they may become oppressive.
	1 Peter 4:3: Non-Christian behavior includes drunkenness.
	Luke 21:34,36: The persons who are drunk when Christ returns will not be ready for His return (No blessings)

God Commands Self Control: (1 Thessalonians 5:6-8)
- Without self-control there is not godliness (2 Timothy 3:3)
  - Without self-control in the Greek is the same as being incontinent.
  - Without self-control in the Greek is being without power.
- Power is living by the Holy Spirit (Galatians 5:16)
  - So I say live by the Spirit, and you will not gratify the desires of the sinful nature.
- Living By The Spirit
  - Allow the Fruit of The Spirit to grow. (Galatians 5:22-23)
    - Fruit starts to grow with the acceptance of Jesus Christ as Lord and Savior.
    - Fruit starts to grow with your faith, and rebirth.
  - Plant in you what will please the Spirit, and not flesh. (Galatians 6:8)
  - When under pressure do a work for the Lord. (Galatians 6:9)
  - Focus your mind on what the Spirit desires. (Romans 8:5)
  - Know, your body will suffer.
  - Know victory is in Christ. (Romans 8:17,18)
  - Seek not being a slave to your flesh.
  - Pray
  - Depend on The Holy Spirit to help during periods of weakness.
  - Know the Godhead is fighting your battle.
    - God is for you. (Romans 8:27)
    - The Holy Spirit is interceding for you. (Romans 8:31)
    - Jesus Christ is interceding for you. (Romans 8:34)

IV. BE ANXIOUS FOR NOTHING
My Anxious Thoughts:

Self Test:

- I am anxious about _____
- I am concerned about _____
- I am distracted by _____
- I am divided by _____
- I am weighed down thinking about _____

The Yoke of Worry:
- Psalms 139:23:
    - Search me, O God, and know my heart;
    - Test me and know my anxious thoughts.
- Unfruitfulness of worry – Luke 21:34
    - Weighs down the heart
    - Saps energy
    - Leads to drunkenness
    - Is like a trap
    - Worry causes the rejection of the Word of Life
        - Matthew 13:22, Mark 4:19; Luke 8:14

    The one who received the see that fell among the thorns is the man who hears the word, but the **worries** of this life and the deceitfulness of wealth choke it, making it unfruitful.
- The Greek term for worry often translated "cares" (KJV)
    - Concerned about the future

- Anxious expectation (Encyclopedia of Bible Words, Richards)
- Healthy Concern – motivated about something which you have control
  - Increases Creativity
  - Promotes Initiative
  - Guides Focusing
  - Directs the mind to the important
- Legitimate Worry:
  - Concern with the Lord's affairs.
  - How to please the Lord (1 Corinthians 7:32)
  - A married person has divided concerns:
    - How to please the wife/husband
    - How to please The Lord simultaneously
  - Members of the body of Christ have concern for each other (1 Corinthians 12:25-26)
  - Pastors are concerned for other churches (2 Corinthians 11:28)
- Unrighteous Worry (Matthew 6:25-34)
  - Worrying about the material things of life.
  - Not living by faith.
  - Worrying about things over which have no control.
  - Worrying about things which non-believers chase.
  - Worrying about tomorrow.
  - Worrying about how will defend yourself before non-believers (Luke 12:11-12)

- Misdirected Worry (Luke 41-42)
    - Worrying about good works rather than spending time with Jesus

    Martha was told by Jesus that she was upset over minor things, but Mary had chosen the better things.

Causes of Worry:
- Misplaced trust.
    - Trusting men whose hearts are no in the Lord.
    - Walking in the flesh.
    - Jeremiah 17:5: Cursed is the one who trusts in man, who depends on flesh for strength, whose heart turns away from the Lord.

Breaking The Yoke:
- Handling the Worry (1 Peter 5:6-9)
    - Cast all your anxiety on Him, because He cares for you.
    - How to Cast:
        - Bait is faith
        - Be humble to God.
        - Be self-controlled through the Holy Spirit.
        - Be alert – know the plows of Satan and the flesh
        - Know that others are in similar situations.
        - Depend on God.
    - Pray (Philippians 4:6)
        - Ask for what is needed
        - Give Thanks
        - Bring peace to your hearts and minds
    - Wait with patience

- o Think truth
- o Think on the good
    - Know patience comes through trials (James 1:3)
    - Be joyful in hope (Romans 12:12)

BIBLIOGRAPHY

Bibles

Amplified Bible. (1987). Grand Rapids, MI: Zondervan Bible Publishers.

Barker, K. (Gen Ed.), (1985) *The NIV Study Bible,* Grand Rapids, MI: Zondervan,

Books

Center for Substance Abuse Services. (1996). *Effective Substance Abuse Counseling With Specific Population Groups.* Michigan Department of Health.

Center for Substance Abuse Services. (1996). *Fundamentals of Alcohol and Other Drug Problems.* Michigan Department of Health.

Hunt, J. (2004). Catch the Thief Hiding in Your Heart. *Biblical Counseling Keys.* Dallas, TX: Hope for the Heart. p. 1-4.

Hunt, J. (2004). God's Word for Worried Hearts. *Biblical Counseling Keys.* Dallas, TX: Hope for the Heart.

Gingrich, F.W. and Danker, F. W. (1958). *A Greek-English Lexicon of the New Testament and Other Early Christian Literature.* Chicago, IL: University of Chicago Press.

Gower, R. (1987). *The New Manners and Customs of the Bible Times.* Chicago, IL: Moody Press.

Laird, C. (1974). *Webster's New World Thesaurus.* New York: Popular Library.

Webster's Seventh New Collegiate Dictionary. (1967). Springfield, MA: G & C Merriam Company Publishers.

Chapter 4
FAILURE OF PRIDE VERSUS POWER OF HUMILITY

Pride and Humility

BSJ Christian Seminars
Minister Brenda Simuel Jackson, Ph.D.
© 2004 All rights reserved.

SEMINAR OBJECTIVES

- Learn the characteristics of unhealthy pride
- Learn the differences between pride and self-esteem
- Understand the power of true humility
- Understand the difference between humbleness and submissiveness

AN HUMBLE MANNER
© Brenda Simuel Jackson

It is not about me.
What can I do?
It is not about me.
What strengths do I possess?
It is not about me.
Praise is not my entitlement?
It is not about me.
What flag represents my concerns?
I humbly bow to my Creator.
All things He can do.
I humbly bow to my Sustainer.
Strength is His due.
I humbly bless His Holy Name.
Praise belongs to Him.
I raise the Blood Stained Banner –
Submitting to Him in an humble manner.

KEY SCRIPTURES

Meditate on the Following Scriptures:
- James 4:1-10 (Submission to God)
- Proverbs 29:23 (Humbleness)
- 2 Timothy 3:2 (Ungodly pride)
- Philippians 2:2-9a (Humility of Christ)
- John 13:2-17 (True Servant/Leader)
- 1 Peter 2:13 - 3:7 (Submission to Rulers, Masters, and other authorities)
- Luke 18:9-14 (Pride versus Humility)

FUEL FOR FAILURE

I. Secular Pride (Webster, 675)
   A. Inordinate self-esteem
   B. Reasonable self-respect
   C. Conceit
   D. Disdain
   E. Ostentatious display
   F. Elation from an act or possession

II. Scriptural Pride
   A. Primary root term is to rise, to grow, to increase
   B. Scriptural metaphors:
     1. Pride, an ascending column of smoke (Isaiah 9:18)
     2. Pride, proud waves (Job 38:11)
     3. Pride, a thicket or jungle of Jordan (Jeremiah 12:5)

   C. Old Testament term for pride is majesty, splendor
     1. An attribute of God's sovereignty (Isaiah 2:10, 19, 21)
     2. An action of God (Psalm 68:34-35)
     3. A characteristic of God (Deuteronomy 33:29b)

   D. Those defeated by pride:
     1. Satan (Ezekiel 28:17ff)
       a. Proud heart
       b. Corrupted wisdom

         c. Many sins
         d. Dishonest trade
         e. Thrown to the earth
         f. Horrible end; to be no more
      2. Moab (Isaiah 16:6-7)
         a. Pride and conceit
         b. Empty boast
         c. Lament
         d. Grieve
      3. Philistines (Zechariah 9:6)
         a. Driven from their land in Ashdod
         b. Driven from the land of Canaan

      4. Assyria (Nahum)
         a. The Lord's anger against Ninevah, capital of Assyria
         b. Nineveh destroyed

III. Pride is sin:
   A. Denies the significance of God
   B. Puts self above others
   C. Type of reprobate mind
   D. Lover of self (2 Timothy 3:2)
   E. Confidence is in other than God (Romans 11:20; 1 Timothy 6:17)
   F. Believe can live successfully apart from obedience to God

IV. Results of Unhealthy Pride:
   A. Does not relate with love
   B. Closes the heart to the Holy Spirit
   C. Prevents being obedient to God's commands
   D. Leads to disgrace (Proverbs 11:2)
   E. Leads to quarrels (Proverbs 13:10)
   F. Leads to destruction (Proverbs 16:18

Share personal testimonies of unhealthy pride.

LIST THE WORDS YOU ARE ABLE TO DISCERN FROM THE TERM
PRIDE

Words of Positive Meaning:	Words with Negative Meaning:
Example: Ripe	**Example: Ire**

CONCEIT SCALE

Select the response that best represents your attitude.

1	2	3	4	5
Strongly Disagree	Disagree	Neutral	Agree	Strongly Agree

1. ____ I am wonderfully made because I am a creation of God.

2. ____ I am not better or worse than my neighbor.

3. ____ I can rejoice at the good fortunes of those who have less education/experience than I.

4. ____ Small gains of a person are just as significant as those who make giant leaps in history.

5. ____ I will not admit my job was fairly eliminated.

6. ____ I am entitled to all the best.

7. ____ I am the best.

8. ____ No one can do my job the way I can.

9. ____ I deserve all the credit for the accomplishments in my life.

10. ____ My material gains in life are a credit to my achievements.

Review your responses and write down those that did not show confidence in God or did not express God's pride in you.

POSITIVE EXPRESSIONS OF PRIDE

- God's works
- Accomplishments of others when God is given the glory.
- Accomplishments of self when God is glorified.
- God's grace
- Total surrender to God.

The Pharisee and The Publican
Luke 18:9-14

SPIRITUAL PRIDE	**GODLY HUMILITY**
Confident of own self-righteousness	Presumes no self-righteousness
Looks down on others	Recognizes unworthiness before God
Does not admit personal sin	Admits personal sin
Sees faults in others	Sees own faults and need for forgiveness
Performs religious deeds before others	Prays for mercy before God
Refuses salvation and exalts	Receives salvation and is exalted by God

LIST THE WORDS YOU ARE ABLE TO DISCERN FROM THE TERM

HUMBLENESS

Words with Positive Meaning:	Words with Negative Meaning:
Example: Bless	Example: Bum

IS IT SELF RESPECT OR IS IT PRIDE

Scriptures:	**Pride**: Unwillingness to submit to God and an insensitivity to others	Scriptures:	Self-Esteem: Is self-respect: For You created my inmost being...I am fearfully and wonderfully made: Your works are wonderful...
Psalm 10:4	Does not seek God Does not think of God	Psalm 139:13-16	Creation of God His marvelous work
Proverbs 6:16,17	Haughty eyes Lying tongue Sheds innocent blood	Psalm 119:1,5,6	Blessed of God No shame Obedient to God's statutes
Proverbs 8:13	Evil behavior Perverse Speech	Matthew 5:3-12	Give mercy Pure heart Peacemaker
Proverbs 11:2	Disgrace	Psalm 119:22	No scorn No contempt
Proverbs 13:10	Fuel for quarrels	Psalm 32:2	Sins not held against me No deceit
Proverbs 16:18	Precedes destruction		
Proverbs 25:6,7	Lifts self	Proverbs 31:18-31	Seek righteousness Industrious
Proverbs 27:2	Praises self		Not lazy Help others Provides for family Conducts business with expertise Has dignity Has wisdom

POWER OF BEING HUMBLE

I. Humbleness
   A. Dependence on Christ

   B. A lowly status

   C. Blessings of an obedient spirit

   D. Evolutionary process in **B**iblical meaning (TWOT)[23]
      1. Changed from being economically powerless
      2. Changed from being socially powerless
      3. Changed to total dependence on a Supreme Being
      4. Changed from one's relationship to society to one's relationship to God
      5. Changed from emphasis on outward character to inward attitude toward God and others

   E. Original Hebraic term had the meaning to be low, to sink (TWOT)
      1. To be humiliated
      2. Forced poverty because of enemies (Encyclopedia, NIV, 346)
      3. Indication of abasement from dislike
      4. Used as a result of leprosy (Leviticus 13:20-21, 26, 14:37-38), (TWOT, 950)
      5. Description of the oppressed
         a. Afflicted
         b. Humble
         c. Gentle (Isaiah 61:1)
      6. Bring into subjection (TWOT)
         a. Bringing recalcitrant people into subjection as was the "stiff necked Hebrew".
         b. Bringing the Spirit into subjection. (TWOT, 445)

   F. Ancient Greek culture meanings:
      1. Someone of low social status
      2. Someone socially powerless

---

[23] Theological Words of the Old Testament (TWOT)

3. Someone of disgrace
   a. Person of shame
   b. Publicly humiliated
      i. Death on the cross (Richards, 347, Luke 1:52, Romans 12:16)
      ii. Held in contempt as was Jesus

G. God humbled His people to bring them to Himself
   1. Genesis 15:13: 400 years of painful treatment of the Israelites
   2. Deuteronomy 8:2: Humbled by being led in the desert 40 years
   3. 1 King 11:39: Chastened by affliction as in the dispersion

II. Scriptural humbleness is position measured against God
   A. In comparison to God, man is lowly
      1. Jesus had to make himself less than God to take on His humanity
      2. He had to take on a servant's nature (attitude)

   B. The Relationship of humbleness to God is one of obedience
      1. Jesus was obedient unto death
      2. Jesus was obedient to death on the cross

   C. Humility guides to self-examination (NIV, 347)
      1. Act of preparation for Communion is out of humbleness
      2. Examine self
      3. Confess sins

   D. Humility is guide to obedience
      1. Do not judge God's Word
      2. Respond to His Word as authority (1 Timothy 3:16-17)
      3. Respond to Christ like a child without question (Matthew 18:1-4)
      4. Respond to Christ with our heart and our minds

   E. Humility guides to relationship with other believers
      1. Use gifts to serve others (Romans 12:3-16)
      2. In serving others, do not think more highly of self than should

3. Consider the interest of others as well as personal interest
4. Consider others better than self
5. Willingly associate with persons of "low" position (Romans 12:10)
6. Prestige is not an issue (Christ is not seeking prestige)

IV. Value of Humbleness
   A. Freedom from personal sense of importance demonstrating dependence on God

   B. Humbleness increases honest concern for others

   C. Humbleness is sign of being chosen by God (Colossians 3:12)
      1. Christian virtue
      2. Response to God
      3. Response to human needs (Richards, Bible Dictionary, 506)
      4. Demonstrates repentance (Leviticus 26:41-2, 2 Chronicles 7:14)
      5. Right relationship with God.

V. Examples: Scriptural and in our culture today of those following a life of humility, putting the interest of others before personal interest
   A. Moses was described as more humble than anyone on earth (Numbers 12:3)
      1. Left a high position for his people
      2. Lived in a desert place
      3. Put concerns of his people before himself and his family
      4. Obedient to God
      5. Dependant on God

   B. Solomon was humble in his request for wisdom and discernment (1 Kings 3:1-15)
      1. Put persons to be judged first
      2. Put wealth and riches last

   C. Hosea
      1. Prophet for 38 years
      2. Humbly obeyed God by taking an adulterous wife

3. Accepted humiliation by standing by his wife

D. Ruth
   1. Put her mother in law first
   2. Depended on God

E. Mother Teresa
   1. Devoted herself to working among the poorest of the poor
   2. Started an order "Missionaries of Charity" to love and care for the nobodies

F. Coretta Scott King
   1. Human Rights Advocate
   2. Did not retire from public life, carried on work of her husband to fulfill his dream of equal rights for all Americans

VI. Jesus, the Christ, Ministry to the Humble
   A. Blessed are the poor in Spirit (attitude of dependence on God for help and comfort)

   B. Matthew 11:29:
      1. Take the yoke of Christ to be joined to Him
      2. Christ made himself humble and lowly
      3. We give our burdens to Him
      4. Yoked together
      5. Pull together
      6. Assume meekness of Christ

VII. Rewards of Humbleness
   A. The Lord saves the humble (Psalm 18:27)

   B. The Lord upholds the cause of the humble (Psalm 147:6)

   C. The Lord gives grace (unmerited favor) to the humble (1 Peter 5:5)

   D. The Lord blesses the humble with well being (Matthew 5:5

E. The humble receive salvation into the Kingdom of God.

   F. The Lord will exalt the humble, raised to place of honor (Luke 14: 8-11)

Conclusion:
"Humble yourselves, therefore under God's mighty hand, that he may lift you up in due time." (1 Peter 5:6 NIV)

The power of humility is the benefit of being a member of the family of Jesus Christ. Let us treat others as Jesus treats us.

REVIEW OF FAILURE AND POWER

I. Pride focuses on self:
    A. Causes us to be disobedient to God

    B. Causes us not to relate to each other with love

    C. Closes down our heart to the teaching of the Holy Spirit

    D. Leads to disgrace

    E. Leads to quarrels

    F. Leads to destruction

II. But, Godly pride focuses on God:
    A. Gives God glory for His work and our redemption

    B. Is delighted in the accomplishments of others

    C. Is pride in what God is doing in our hearts

    D. Is pride of God's grace, our salvation

    E. Is totally surrender to God

III. The antithesis of unholy pride is the Christian virtue of humbleness and Godly humility:
   A. A relationship to God, accepting Him as Lord

   B. Being obedient to God

   C. Knowing His is authority

   D. Following Jesus without question

   E. Examining self and confessing our sins

   F. Using our gifts in the service of others with the attitude of a servant

   G. While serving others, not thinking of self more highly than we ought.

BIBLIOGRAPHY AND SUGGESTED BOOKS

Harris, R. Laird, Archer, Jr, Gleason L. and Waltke, Bruce K. *Theological Wordbook of the Old Testament, Volumes 1 &2*. Chicago, IL: Moody Press, 1980.

Richards, Lawrence O. *The Revell Bible Dictionary*. New Jersey: Fleming H. Revell Co., 1990.

Webster's Seventh New Collegiate Dictionary. Massachusetts: G & C Merriam Company Publishers. 1967

Chapter 5
FRUIT: SPIRITUALLY SWEET, EMOTIONALLY MATURE

Fruit of a Believer

BSJ Christian Seminars
Minister Brenda Simuel Jackson, Ph.D.
© 2004 All rights reserved.

MY FRUIT
©Brenda Simuel Jackson

Through the fruitfulness of love,
I resisted refusing a kind word to my enemy.

Through the joy of my fruit,
praise was the harvest even during the struggles.

Fruitful peace calmed my spirit
and maintained a wholesomeness of focus.

The sweet taste of patience continued to last
and cultivate genuinely true relations.

The sharp poignant kindness and goodness
helped the taste of patience to last longer, and
soothing faithfulness taught me how more like Christ I long to know.

Treating all I encounter with respect and gentleness
gives the lasting fragrance requiring custom pruning of the
Master Gardner.

Self-control brought a fresh new taste,
enhancing the life of being part of a fruit filled field.

SEMINAR OBJECTIVES

- Achieve understanding that the fruit of the Spirit is a result of relationships

- Understand the relationship between repentance and spiritual fruit

- Evaluate the correlation between emotional health and evidence of spiritual fruit

- Learn to recognize spiritual fruit

- Know the difference between being self-controlled and Spirit controlled

REVELATION SCRIPTURES

- Galatians 5:16-26
- James 3:17-18

THE FRUIT OF GRACE
(Romans 7:4-5)[24]

- Evidence of Rebirth
    - Widow released from ties of deceased spouse
    - Released from condemnation of the law.
    - Free to start a new life
    - Free to marry grace
        - Grace of God
        - From this union fruit will come
- The law points out desires of flesh (candy in a candy store)
- Unity of character of the Lord
    - Only one who is spiritually alive can bear fruit
    - Only one who is spiritually alive can live holy.
- Inward divine power produces fruit
- Controlled by the Spirit
    - Only the believer has the option of living by the Spirit
        - The law says speed limit 65mph
        - The flesh says, I have a smooth ride with a HEMI
        - Choices
            - Cruise at 75 – 80 mph
            - Cruise at 65 mph
    - Married to the world, fruit is worthless

I. Fruitfulness: (Ephesians 4:1-4)
- Interpersonal relationship with Jesus
    - How to relate to other believers
    - How to handle personal life

- Must live by His words
    - How do you turn the other cheek?
    - Do not retaliate, seek peace
    - Commit the case to the Lord

---

[24] In Radmacher, Earl D. et.al ,*Nelson's New Illustrated Bible Commentary*, Nashville, Thomas Nelson, "…Out of intimacy with Christ comes the fruit of practical righteousness…only believers can walk according to the Spirit.", 1436 –7.

- Know God will judge "Who, when He was reviled did not revile in return; when He suffered. He did not threaten, but committed Himself to Him, Who judges righteously." (1 Peter 2:23)

- Living the Word (Bible Knowledge Commentary)
    - Humility promotes unity (not weakness)
    - Gentleness and meekness are opposite of rudeness and harshness
    - Patience is enduring through adversity
    - With right attitude there is unity
    - With right attitude there is peace

- Elements of Unity
    - One Body – Universal Church
    - One Spirit (Holy Spirit) indwelling the Church (Ephesians 4:4-6)
    - One Lord – Christ, the Head of the Church

GROUP EXERCISE

Fill in the blank	Fill in the blank
FRUIT OF MY FLESH	**FRUIT OF THE INDWELLED SPIRIT**
• Date: _____ Day:	• Date: _____ Day:
I lied (example)	I forgave a wrong against me. (example)
I was stubborn	I was patient
I was hardheaded	I endured
I _____	I _____
I _____	I _____
I _____	I _____
I _____	I _____

REPENTANCE NEEDS

FRUIT OF A SINFUL NATURE	FRUIT OF THE SPIRIT
Sexual immorality	Love
Impurity	Joy
Debauchery	Peace
Idolatry and witchcraft	Patience
Hatred	Kindness
Discord	Goodness
Jealousy	Faithfulness
Fits of Rage	Gentleness
Selfishness	Self-Control
Selfish Ambition	
Dissensions	
Factions	
Drunkenness	
Orgies	
The Like	

- True Change (Acts 26:20; Philippians 3:13,14)
    - Repentance
        - Past not identified
        - Future not be worried about
        - Deal with the present
    - Fruit of Repentance (Luke 3:8)
        - Change of mind
            - About Jesus Christ
            - Commitment to Jesus
            - Turning to God
        - Adopted of God
        - Turn from evil (sin)
        - Follows God
        - Change in attitude

- - - o Bitter Fruit – The vineyard does not produce
- Cries of distress (Isaiah 5:1-6)
    - Loss of God's protection
    - Briars and thorns in your life
    - No fruit of righteousness
    - Desolation in the field
    - Fruit of The Prodigal Son
        - Group Exercise
            - Describe your ***hog pen***
            - Why did you leave it?
            - Where did you go when you left?
            - What did you find?

II. Relationship Fruit
- Fruit of light in the Lord (Ephesians 5:8-10)
    - Goodness
    - Righteousness
    - Truth
    - What pleases the Lord (Ask the group the question)
- Fruit of discipline (Hebrew 12:11)
    - Righteousness
        - Glory to God
        - Praise to God (Philippians 1:11)
    - Peace

WHAT IS THE FRUIT OF THE SPIRIT

I. A New Creation (2 Corinthians 5:17)[25]

---

[25] "Therefore if anyone is in Christ, he is a new creation, the old has gone, the new has come."

SPIRITUAL FRUIT - Galatians 5:22-23

FRUIT[26]	SCRIPTURES	DESCRIPTIONS	APPLICATIONS
Love	Galatians 5:22	Produced by The Holy Spirit	Living Christlike; love is the foundation of grace.
	1 John 4:7-8,12	God is Love. Love one another.	Whoever loves has been born of God, whoever does not love, does not know God.
	Romans 5:5; 12:9-10	God's love ministered to the believer by The Holy Spirit; sincerity, Humility, Commitment.	Be fervent in service for The Lord; show social concern for one another; show no hypocrisy.
	1 Corinthians 13:4-7	Equals patience, equals kindness, doesn't envy, doesn't boast; is not proud; is not rude; is not self-seeking; is not easily angered; keeps no record of wrongs; does not like evil, has joy with truth; protects, trusts, is hope, is perseverance.	When wronged does not retaliate, does not seek self-satisfaction, does not rush to litigation[27], watches how communication occurs in service, remains stedfast even in unpleasant situations, demonstrates God's love, does not seek to do harm.
	2 Corinthians 8:24	Love has action.	
	Galatians 5:13-14	Serve others not self.	Giving to those in need. Guard against self righteousness
	1 Peter 4:8	Love strenuously, sacrificing for others, accepting their faults.	Sacrificing for others regardless of faults.

---

[26] Healthy change in desires, actions, and sense of self because of a relationship with Christ.

[27] In application, must view in the context of what was happening in the Corinthian Church: Taking each other to court, poor treatment of the poor during communion, division, and condoning sin, incest.

Joy	Galatians 5:22; John 15:9-11	Inner rejoicing because of a relationship with Christ.	The joy of Christ within the believer is manifested in obedience.
	Luke 10:21	Jesus brings joy through the Holy Spirit	Joy is produced from within, and is not the external signs we see of laughter or happiness in materials things.
	Psalm 16:11	Joy is in the presence of God. Joy is a relationship with God.	Living a life that leads to God's eternal presence.
	Deuteronomy 16:15	Joy in God's provisions; joy in God's deliverance.	Celebration of our salvation, and of God's blessings.
	1 Chronicles 16:1-36	David rejoices by Thanking God through brunt offerings, fellowship offerings, and writing psalm.	Thanking God demonstrates our inner joy for all He has done, is , and will do.
	Psalm 19:8a	Joy in God's Word	Righteousness brings inner joy, which we receive from the Word of God.
	Psalm 119:14	Obedience to God's Word brings joy.	Our richness is in God's word.
	Romans 14:16-17	Kingdom of God is righteousness, peace & joy in The Holy Spirit, do not allow your good to be evil spoken of.	The Kingdom of God is within the believer, joy is in serving Christ.
	Acts 16:34	The jailer was filled with joy because he and his family elieved.	Salvation is joy.
	Acts 13:49-52	Paul; and Barnabus expelled from the region because of the	Perseverance is continued with inner joy through the Holy Spirit which is a result of the Gospel.

	2 Corinthians 7:2-4	Word. In times of trouble, Paul continues to have joy.	This time of testing of our faith is to build perseverance and brings joy.
	Philippians 1:25-26; 2:1-2	Faith brings joy; united with Christ brings joy.	Encouragement because of relationship with Christ.
Peace	Galatians 5:22; Romans 1:7; 1Corinthians 1:3	A gift of Christ	Inner repose even in adverse circumstances.
	Ephesians 2:14-18	Peace is unity	In Christ, there is no division, all believers have been reconciled back to God, there is one Spirit.
	Ephesians 4:3	Unity of The Spirit	Singleness of Spirit through the bond (reconciliation) of peace (Jesus The Christ)
	1 Corinthians 14:33	God is not a God of Disorder but of peace.	Through Christ, there is order and harmony.
	2 Timothy 2:22	Pursue righteousness, faith, love, and peace; call on the Lord out of a pure heart.	Peace is a commitment to harmony.
	Colossians 3:12-15	The peace of Christ rules our character.	The attitude of peace is of compassion kindness, humility, gentleness, patience, the results of the action of the Holy Spirit, causes us

	Matthew 10:34	Peace with Christ causes conflict with others.	to forgive others as Christ has forgiven us.
	Mark 5:34	Being healed, going in peace	Christ is first in our lives, peace with Christ, is conflict with those against Christ.
	John 14:27	Peace of Christ, inner peace that lets the believer face danger and suffering without fear.	Enjoy being content and rest in God's healing.
	John 16:33	Although trouble in the world, the believer has inner peace, through the victory of Christ.	In unity with Christ, there is no fear of the future; Christ is not physically beside us, but His peace is in us. Face troubles of this world knowing our future is secure.
Longsuffering[28]	Galatians 5:22	Forbearance when provoked.	Does not retaliate when wronged.
	Romans 2:4	Provide opportunity for repentance.	Provides time for change from wrong actions to God's way.

---

[28] Quality of self restraint in the face of provocation which does not hastily retaliate or promptly punish, is associated with mercy, (Vines, 377).

Kindness[29]	Galatians 5:22; Romans 11:22	Opposite of judgment	Accept the benevolence (salvation) of God.
	Ephesians 2:7	God's Grace	God's favor to give salvation to the believer.
	Titus 3:4	God saved us because of His mercy. He saved us through the washing of m rebirth of and renewal by The Holy Spirit Whom He poured out on us through Jesus Christ.	God's moral goodness in us enables us to be kind to others.
	Luke 6:35	Loving and being kind to our enemies, lending with no expectation of return	Follow Christ who is kind to the ungrateful and the wicked.
	Ephesians 4:32	Forgiving	Through forgiving each other, we are kind to one another.
Goodness	Galatians 5:22	Morally honorable, and reaching out to others	Doing good to others even when not deserved
	Luke 8:8	Being good soil.	Having a character with beneficial effects.

---

[29] Kindness is faithfulness to a relationship…to act in a loyal, loving way to a person. (Richards, 375)

Faith[30]	Galatians 5:22	Justification through Christ.	Quality of trustworthiness
	Romans 3:25; 2 Corinthians 1:24	Firm persuasion or conviction on hearing the Gospel	Faith in One Who is reliable which causes us to be faithful servants.
	John 1:12; 2 Corinthians 5:7	Surrender to Christ and gain in relationship to God	Our conduct exhibits our surrender
	Matthew 24:45; 25:21-23	Servanthood	Good Stewardship
	1 Corinthians 4:2	Faithful in the trust received	Faithful servants
Meekness[31]	Galatians 5:23; James 1:21	Humbly accept the Word planted within.	Submissive to God's word.
	Matthew 5:5	The humble are already blessed.	Recognize our relations to God; our lowly estate when compared to God.
	1 Peter 3:4	Inner beauty of a quiet spirit	Submissiveness
	James 3:13	Learned humility	Using wisdom and understanding in acting humbly.
	1 Peter 3:15	Speaking in gentleness	Show respect when defending the reasons for having hope
		A condition of the mind and heart, shows our attitude toward God.	

---

[30] A main element in Faith is relationship to the invisible God. (Vines, 222)

[31] Meekness is humbleness, gentleness, attitude that maintains patience despite offenses.

Self-Control	Galatians 5:23	Self-mastery	Curbing fleshly desires
	2 Peter 1:6	Making your calling sure by adding to your faith.	
	Titus 1:8	Disciplined	Inner strength to control desires and actions.

Note: The Greek terminology is the basis for each of the descriptive context outlined in the chart.

I. Out of the overflow of his heart, his mouth speaks: (Luke 6:45) – MORE SPIRITUAL FRUIT
   - One's character is betrayed by one's words
   - Man must give an account for every careless word spoken (Matthew 12:36)
   - By your words you will be acquitted
   - By your words you will be condemned (Matthew 12:37)

II. Human actions and words are fruit of a person's character

III. IS YOUR FRUIT RIPE? MATURE? (Read Matthew 7:16 – 20)
   - _____ Your doctrine?
   - _____ Your character?
   - _____ What is stored in your heart?
   - _____ Your actions?
   - _____ Where are you leading others?
   - Are you a thorn-bush? (Preventing good deeds?)

IV. Healthy cultivation of Your fruit (McMinn, 45)
   - Fight self-centeredness
   - During trials:
     o Experience grace
     o Experience hope
   - Develop a healthy self-image
   - Without Jesus, there is no fruit (John 15:5-8)
     o Jesus, the Vine
       - Branch
       - Bear Fruit
     o Disciple
   - Accurate sense of self allows the recognition of responsibility to God, (McMinn, 44)
     o Responsibility to others
     o Responsibility to self.
   - Cannot manifest Fruit of Spirit without healthy Spiritual concept of self

MOTIVATION AND SPIRITUAL MATURITY

The fruit of the Spirit aids in realizing the unmet needs in our lives. Motivation reaches its human peak through "self-actualization" (Abraham H. Maslow). To self actualize spiritually is to be motivated by recognizing Who is the source of meeting all unmet needs. This is a side product of the Spirit's fruit.

Motivational Ladder

Ladder Position	Maslow's Hierarchy	God's Provisions
Top rung #5	Self-Actualization: Reaching the height of one's abilities.	1 John 5:14-15 Being in the Will of God, purposeful living. 1 Corinthians 12:1-30 Spiritual gifts. God gives talents. Philemon 10-12 Being useful Galatians 4:1-7,31;5:1 Being set free
#4	Self Esteem: Desire for recognition and self-respect.	Psalm 139: 13-16 I am somebody. Genesis 1:26, I am made in the image of God, Ephesians 2:1-9 I have been forgiven my sins, I have been given what it takes to be successful as was Nehemiah, Paul, timothy, Deborah, Lydia, and others.
#3	Love/Acceptance: The need to belong, to be a part of.	John 3:16 God loves me; I am adopted into the family of God, and I am a joint heir with Jesus Christ. Ephesians 9:4, Galatians 4:5 He will never forsake me. We have fellowship.
#2	Safety/Security: Desire to be free from violence, harm disease.	Psalm 61:3-4 He provides refuge, 2 Timothy 1:7, provides power, sound mind, and judgment; Philippians 4:7, Gives peace of mind, Ephesians 1:4, 1:7, security in our salvation.
1st rung #1	Physiological: Biological needs	Manna, water at Meriba, Physical healings are example of needs met. Today as with Christ, and with Paul, jobs, education and training, given and received.

SPIRITUAL AND PSYCHOLOGICAL FRUIT[32]

Fruit of The Spirit Galatians 5:22-23	Characteristics of Self-Actualizers	Desires of Self-Actualizers
Love	Profound Relationships	Unity, Beauty
Joy	Spontaneity, Peak Experiences, Continued freshness of appreciation	Aliveness, Playfulness
Peace	Fellowship with humanity, Acceptance of self and others	Simplicity
Patience		Individuality; Richness
Kindness	Unhostile sense of humor	Justice
Goodness	Efficient perception of reality	Goodness, Values, Truth
Faithfulness		Completion
Gentleness		Balance, harmony
Self-Control	Autonomy, Task-Centered	

---

[32] McMinn, Ph.D, Mark R. *Psychology, Theology, and Spirituality in Christian Counseling*, Wheaton, Ill.
　　Tyndale-House Publishers, Inc. 1996.

BIBLIOGRAPHY

BIBLES

Barker, Kenneth, Gen Ed. *The NIV Study Bible, New International Version,* Grand Rapids, MI: Zondervan, 1985.

Berry, George Ricker. *Interlinear Greek-English New Testament with Greek- English Lexicon.* Grand Rapids: Baker Book House, 1993.

REFERENCES:

Adams, Jay E. *The Christian Counselor's Manual.* Grand Rapids: Baker Book House, 1973.

Brown, Francis, Driver, S.R. & Briggs, Charles. *A Hebrew and English Lexicon of The Old Testament.* Oxford: Clarendon Press, 1930.

Harris, R., Laird, Archer J., Gleason, Waltke, Bruce K. *Theological Wordbook of the Old Testament.* Volume 2, Chicago: Moody Press, 1980

Maslow, Abraham H. "A Theory of Human Motivation," *Psychological Review,* 50 (1943), 370-96.

McMinn, Ph.D. Mark D. *Psychology, Theology, and Spirituality in Christian Counseling.* Wheaton, Ill. Tyndale House Publishers, Inc. 1996.

Richards, Lawrence O. *New International Encyclopedia of Bible Words, based on the NIV and the NASB.* Grand Rapids: Zondervan Publishing House, 1991.

Packer, J.I., Tenny, Merrill C., & White, Williams, Jr. *Nelson's Illustrated Encyclopedia of Bible Facts.* Volume 1. Boston: Halo Press, 1995.

Vine, W.E., Unger, Merrill F., White, Jr. William. *Vine's Complete Expository Dictionary of Old and New Testament Words.* Nashville, TN: Thomas Nelson Publishers, 1985.

PRAYER POWER
© Brenda Simuel Jackson

Blessed with a new day is reason to say Thank You Lord,
    even before feet hit the floor, This is Prayer – With my Father.

Seeking His strength in rough moments during life's day,
    a cry out, Lord help, Prayer – With my Father.

Through silent tears, feeling His presence and comfort,
    This too, Prayer – With my Father.

Asking for help, protection, deliverance, for those I love,
    those I don't love, even self, Yes – Prayer – With my Father.

Praise God! He is God, there is none like Him; He demonstrated His love
for me through the perfect sacrifice, a prayer of praise?
    Prayer – With my Father.

Sitting still, listening, hearing His answer,
    Prayer – With my Father.

Oh, the awesome power of prayer, when prayed to the Only One, to
Whom we should pray, in the Powerful name of Him Who has all power,
    Prayer Power – With my Father, through His Son.

Chapter 6
PRAYER POWER

Communicating with God

BSJ Christian Seminars
Minister Brenda Simuel Jackson, Ph.D.
© 2004 All rights reserved.

SEMINAR OBJECTIVES

- Understanding of what is prayer
- Understand the purposes of prayer
- Knowledge of methods of preparation for prayer
- Knowledge of praying without ceasing.
- Review of Scriptural prayers of intercession
- Knowledge of differences between public prayer and private prayer
- Scriptural commands to pray

Model[33] of Keys To Prayer
(Brenda Simuel Jackson)

GOD

JESUS CHRIST[34]

Receiver Sender

SCRIPTURES

Encodes Decodes

The Holy Spirit[35]

Sender Receiver

THE PRAYING PERSON

---

[33] A process of communication between The Father and a person.

[34] All prayer is in the name of Jesus, John 14:13; If you ask anything in my name, I will do it.

[35] The Holy Spirit interprets what's in the heart of the prayer, Romans 8:26; The Holy helps our weakness, for we do not know how to pray, but the Spirit Himself, intercedes…

SUMMARY KEYS FOR PRAYER

I. Relationship with God
   - Praying only in time of need is like calling relative only at Christmas
   - Being a child of the King is a relationship with God
   - Christ made the way for the relationship
   - Note what happened in Daniel's life – prayed three times a day (Daniel 6:1-28)

II. What is Prayer:
   - Praise to God
   - Talking with God
   - A dialog between two who love each other
   - A discourse of our total dependence on God concerning all our efforts
   - Fellowship with God, the Channel for blessings and power of the Holy Spirit
   - A cry that ends with life
   - Weakness plugged into strength (I can't, but God Can!)

III. God hears and answers prayers:
   - Praying is not a mind exercise
   - Prayer is not a form of self meditation to get deep into oneself
   - Prayer is not to sound good before others
   - God answers prayers:
     o David received forgiveness (Psalm 32:5)
     o Hannah a son (1 Samuel 1:11, 19, 20)
     o The author, a job, education, healings
     o You _____.
   - Sometimes God's answer is no. (Matthew 26:37-42)
     o Jesus' request was not given
     o Not my will but Your will be done
     o We must accept the will of the Father

IV. Prayers should not simply be "gimme".
- Praise and honor for Who God is
- Confession of sins
- Thanksgiving for His mercy and blessings.
- Petitions for others and self (Psalm 63:1-8; Psalm 51; Romans 1:21; James 4:2,3)

V. The fuel for the power of our prayers is faith
- Must believe God can do whatever we are asking
- Must believe His promises
- Must believe in Jesus, The Christ, and the power of the Holy Spirit
- We cannot expect answered prayers if we have not honored His request for obedience (Psalm 37:5, James 1:6,7; 1 John 3:22; Psalm 37:4)

VI. Before we petition, we must deal with sin in our lives.
- Jesus Christ is our High Priest
- Jesus Christ is interceding for us

VII. Prayer Requirements:
- Perseverance
- Patience
- Humility in knowing to Whom we are talking
- Boldness in talk
- Confidence in our Father (1 Corinthians 15:58; Psalm 51:16,17; John 4:10)
- Focus on God not self in prayer
- Use the heart and the brain (Matthew 6:7)
- Take time to listen and hear God, Wait on Him (Psalm 27:14; Hebrews 3:15)
- Sincerity
- Know when to fast

KEYS OF PRAYER

GOD'S PROMISES	REASONS FOR PRAYER	INSTRUCTIONS FOR PRAYER	RELATIONSHIP BUILDING WITH OUR FATHER
Through scriptures, there is identification with God's promises.	**Confession**: Romans 10:8-9 – Identification with the blessing. Psalm 32:1-2 – An open invitation to pray!	Watch and pray (Mark 14:38) keeping awake with spiritual alertness, in an awakened state.	Revelation through Jesus Christ. The Word, Logos (John 1:1-4)
Through Identification, there is a spiritual experience	**Intercession:** Scriptures tell us to pray for one another (James 5:16). Ephesians 1:15-20, Healing from weaknesses.	Pray without ceasing; never miss an opportunity to pray. (1 Thessalonians 5:17)	Revelation of God through the Spoken word (Rhema), Scriptures, 1 Peter 1:23.
Our attention is drawn to God.	**Examples:** Jesus Christ – Mediator and Intercessor (Hebrews 5:1 & 7:25), Paul, Spiritual understanding (Ephesians 1:16-18), Timothy for the peace and dignity of the believer (1 Timothy 2:1-2).	Have a definite time, planned prayer, illustrated by the word, *when*, in Matthew 6:6, Psalm 55:17.	Understanding our relationship to our Father, Galatians 4:4-6. **God is saying Talk with Me.**
1 John 1:9; confess is to identify with the conviction of the Holy Spirit (Matthew 12:31), and the revelation through the Holy Spirit.	**Praise:** The works of God, Who He is, (Revelation 19:1,6; Psalm 33,) Creator, Preserver (Psalm 34), Provider, Deliver, The Good Shepherd (Psalm 23)	Have a special place for prayer (Matthew 6:6, Psalm 55:8).	Increases our confidence in knowing how God will respond. (1 John 5:10-14)

	Thanks: Thanks for what God has done. Psalm 107	Know to Whom we are praying (Matthew 6:9ff, Our Father Who is in Heaven)	We go boldly before the Father through scripture, (Deuteronomy 8:3, Luke 4:4). Man shall not live by bread alone but by every word that proceeds from the mouth of the Lord.
	Supplication: Specific petitions for a particular need (2 Thessalonians 3:1)	Praying with the Illumination of the Holy Spirit – Understanding (1 Corinthians 14:14-15)	Through scripture, the spiritual eye is opened to be in tune to the Lord's Will and His Promises.
	Worship includes prayer	Pray with honesty, and not for show. (Matthew 6:5-7)	Increased understanding of the Person of God, Praying the names of God: Jehovah – "I Am Who I Am", The Self existent One (Exodus 3:14-15 Jehovah Yireh – God will provide (Genesis 22:8-14) Jehovah Nissi, My Banner (Exodus 17:15), Jehovah Shalom – Peace (Judges 6:24), Jehovah My Shepherd (Psalm 23:1) Jehovah, Our Righteousness (Jeremiah 23:6) Jehovah Who heals (Exodus 15:26), Jehovah Eloheim, The Mighty One (Judges 5:3) Adonai, Lord

			Master (Exodus 4:10-12), El Elyon, Most High (Genesis 14:18), El Roi, The Mighty One Who sees (Genesis 16:13), El Shaddai, All Sufficient (Genesis 17:1-20), El Olam, Everlasting (Genesis 21:33), Yeshua, Jesus, Savior (Matthew 16:13-16), Emanuel – God With Us
	God gives us reasons to pray; To *exalt* us as we go humbly before Him, because He cares for us (1Peter 5:6-7), *Not To Worry*, Philippians 4:6, *To glorify the Father* (John 15: 7-8)		
	Recognition of **how dependent** we are on the Father		

"O give thanks unto the Lord, call upon His name: make known His deeds among the people. Sing unto Him, sing psalms unto Him: talk ye of all His wondrous works. Glory ye in His Holy Name: Let the heart of them rejoice that seek the Lord. Seek the Lord, and His strength; seek His face evermore. (Psalm 105:1-4, KJV).

FASTING

Fasting was a common behavior among the Jews, and it was continued by the Christians. The behavior became a ritual, and in New Testament times the ultra religious (Pharisees), fasted twice a week (Luke 18:12).
Historians believe that fasts did not go beyond twice a week because it

was believed to be injurious to one's health. (Freeman, 420). The two days themselves were symbolic. One, the second day of the week, supposedly represents the day Moses went up on Mount Sinai to receive God's written law, and the second day, the fifth day of the week, represents the day of the week Moses came down from Mount Sinai and found Israel in idolatry. Taking the practice to the extremes prompted Jesus to criticize ritual fasting (Matthew 6:16-18). In Zechariah 7:1-7 and 8:19, God questioned the motive for fasting, is it for self or is it for God?

I. Definition of Fasting:
- Vητεια, nesteia, abstinence from food (Matthew 6:16)
- Ασφαλιζω, asfalidzo, to render secure – make fast (Acts 16:24)
- Abstinence, "Use of control over one's body in a way that is holy and honorable (1 Thessalonians 4:3)
- (tsumwm, tsoom), to cover over the mouth.

II. Reasons to Fast:

SCRIPTURES	CONTEXT OF EVENTS	DESCRIPTIONS OF THE FAST	PURPOSES OF THE FAST
Leviticus 16:29; Jeremiah 36:6	Ordinance from God of a ritual when offering sacrifices for sins committed. This was stated after Aaron's two sons died bringing strange fire before the Lord.	Offer sacrifice of self, household, and then for the people. The priest **abstained from eating** on that day, sunup to sunset (1 day), and did **no work**; this was once a year. The people **read from the scroll, the words of the Lord.**	To **cleanse** (repent) from sin
2 Chronicles 20:3	Jehoshaphat was faced with a vast army which could over take the people.	Jehosaphat proclaimed a **national fast** (all persons were to fast), for Judah. All stood in the assembly as Jehoshaphat **prayed** to God.	**Preparation** to make inquiry of the Lord about this army.
1 Samuel 7:5-6	Israel had turned from God and was worshipping idols, and was in the hands of the Philistines. This was a national crisis.	Israel after twenty years **turning back** to the Lord, and Samuel was going to **intercede** with the Lord for their sins. Israel was assembled at Mizpah.	**Preparation** to confess sins, and to **intercede** with God.
1 Samuel 7:2-9		The Israelites fasted for a day and confessed their sins. Samuel offered a suckling lamb and prayed.	The Lord Answered. (see 1 Samuel 7:5-6)
Deuteronomy 9:9	Moses on the Mountain to receive communication, covenant from God for Israel.	Moses stayed on the Mountain 40 days and 40 nights, and ate no food and drank no water.	**Preparation to receive God's word.**
Deuteronomy 9:18-21, 25-26	Moses returns to the top of the mountain to seek forgiveness because of Israel's sin, building a calf and worshipping it.	Moses was **prostrate** before the Lord, fasted until evening, presented burnt offerings and **fellowship** offerings to the Lord.	**To intercede** for Israel to the Lord, not to destroy Israel.

SCRIPTURES	CONTEXT OF EVENTS	DESCRIPTIONS OF THE FAST	PURPOSES OF THE FAST
Judges 20:26, 24-29	The tribe of Benjamin had sinned against a Levite (murdered his wife), and Israel went to war against them as directed by the Lord.	**Israelites weeping** before the Lord, fasted until evening, presented burnt offering and **fellowship** offering to the Lord.	**To seek direction** from God as to whether they should continue in battle against their brother tribe.
1 Samuel 1:3-7	Hannah who was barren, was often provoked by her rival.	Hannah was so **emotionally upset** she would weep and not eat.	Hannah's fast was because she was **downhearted**. She was in crisis.
2 Samuel 13:15-18	David was being punished for his sin against Uriah, and his first sin by Bathsheba was ill.	David **fasted,** spent nights **lying on the ground.** He did this for seven days, as long as the child was alive, as he pleaded with God for the child.	To **plead with God** for the child's life.
Daniel 6:16-20	King Darius has put Daniel in the lion's den, because Daniel had disobeyed a decree.	King Darius, not a Jew, spent **the night without eating, without entertainment and he could not sleep.** The King had prayed, May your God rescue you.	The King **could not** save Daniel and wanted God to save Daniel.
Esther 4:15-17	There was a conspiracy by Haman to kill all the dispersed Jews.	Mordicai had told the Queen who was Jewish that she could help save her people. Queen Esther requested a three day fast night and a day, before going before the King on behalf of her people. Her life was in danger.	The Queen **gathered strength to risk** her life for her people.
Job 3:13	Job had lost his health, all his family, all he owned, including his status and position.	His three friends came to sympathize with him and **refrained from speaking for seven days and seven nights.**	**To sympathize with suffering.**

SCRIPTURES	CONTEXT OF EVENTS	DESCRIPTIONS OF THE FAST	PURPOSES OF THE FAST
Nehemiah 9:1	The Israelites had returned to Jerusalem to rebuild the City, the Gates and the Temple. When Nehemiah arrived he found that restoration was not taking place, the word and the building were being neglected.	**The word was read,** and the people gathered together in **mourning,** sackcloth and ashes to separate from foreigners, **confess** sins, And read from the Book of the Law. **Stood** and **praised** the Lord.	To **confess and to repent** of sins, and to read God's word.
Jonah 3:5,7-9	Jonah preached judgment to the Ninevites. Ninevah is the capitol of Assyria, the nation that was a fierce warrior, and had captured Israel.	Ninevah believed the message, including the King, they went into **mourning,** and the King forbid anyone to taste anything, told the people **not to eat or drink** as they **called urgently on God, and repented,** hoping that God would show compassion.	**Repented** in calling on God.
Matthew 4:1-11	Jesus was baptized and God was well pleased. He was led by the Holy Spirit into the desert where he would be tempted by Satan.	**Jesus fasted forty days and forty nights, and he was hungry,** and now Satan comes to tempt the Lord.	**Preparing the Body and the will for testing,** where reliance is not on self but on the Word of God.

Read Isaiah 58:1-14 and discuss the attitude of fasting.

III. Characteristics of Fasting – A humble character and attitude
- Isaiah 58 – A fast that denies self for the benefit of others
- Loose the chains of injustice (v6)
- Untie the cords of a yoke
- Set the oppressed free
- Share food with the hungry
- Provide the wanderer with shelter
- Clothe the naked
- Do not turn from your own flesh and blood

ARMOR OF GOD ENABLES PRAYER
(Ephesians 6:14-18)

I. Armor of God necessary for effective prayer.
- Attacks of the enemy require armor
- Attacks of the enemy require prayer

II. Preparing for battle:
- Truth, the first piece of armor
  - Truth, the sense of real, ideal, genuine
  - Truth is of God (John 7:28)
  - Truth is of Jesus Christ (John 1:9; 3:33)
  - Preparing for the days battles, require prayer referencing God's truths
  - Truth describes you in your praying:
    - Attitude of truth
    - Character of truth
- Righteousness, is the second piece of armor
  - Righteousness protects the heart
  - Praying in harmony with obligations to God
  - Praying in harmony with obligations to fellow saints (1 Samuel 24:17)
- Praying the name of Jesus, who is our righteousness
- Peace is the third piece of armor,
  - Peace provides steadiness in prayer
  - In harmony with God during prayer
  - Thankful for the good news during prayer

- Faith the next part of the armor:
  - Several types of faith
    - Intellectual faith has no concrete action (Matthew 7:26)
    - Faith of miracles but not of Jesus (Matthew 17:20)
    - Temporary faith (Luke 8:13)
    - True saving faith – pray with true faith (Romans 10:9)
- Salvation – hope the next part of armor (Hebrew 2:1; John 3:16; Romans 6:23)
- Praying the Word of God is the final piece of armor.
  - The Word is a lamp unto our feet
  - The Word is a light unto our path (Psalm 119:105)
- Final Preparation:
  - Prayer in the Spirit
  - Being alert in prayer (Ephesians 6:18)

DRAWING CLOSE TO GOD
STANDING IN HIS PRESENCE
(James 4:7-12; Psalms 25)

I. Drawing close to God:
   - Be humble
   - Confess sins
   - Trust in the Lord
   - Envision God's holiness, His glory, His majesty
   - Think on His attributes
   - Praise Him
   - Think of His concern for you (Psalm 8:4)

II. Psalm 25 teaches how to go to the Lord:
   - Review verses 1-11
     - We go to the Lord in trust
     - We go to the Lord without shame
     - We go to the Lord seeking His guidance
     - We go to the Lord seeking His forgiveness
     - We go to the Lord recognizing His goodness
     - We go to the Lord desiring to be completely God's vessel

- Analysis and Discussion:
  - V1-3 – Trust and no shame
  - v4-7 Seeking God's ways
    - Seeking His truth
    - Seeking His forgiveness
  - v8-11- God is good
  - What did David ask for which revealed his desire to be completely God's?
  - Your answer:

- Application: Seek God's guidance in our prayers
  - How do you know David was in the habit of talking to God and sharing his life with Him?
  - Your answer:

- Application: If God is our Savior, we talk with Him regularly.
  - How did David describe God?
  - Your answer:

- Application: There should be no reasons why we will not go to God.
  - What are the characteristics of persons whom the Lord will teach?
  - Your answer:

- Application: For answered prayer, we must confess our sins
  - We must humble ourselves before Him
  - We must follow His ways

III. Positions for Prayer:
- There is no one position necessary in prayer to be close to the Lord.
- God seeks sincerity.
- God seeks humbleness in approaching the throne of grace

Sample Positions of Prayer in the Bible

Scriptures	Position	Place	Who	Why	Results
Luke 22:41	Knelt on his knees	Mt. Of Olives	Jesus	Agony, fervency	Angel strengthened Him
John 11:41 –42	Raised His eyes	Tomb of Lazarus	Jesus	Thanksgiving	God hears Him
Matthew 26:39	Fell on His face	Garden of Gethsemane	Jesus	Grieved, distress at pending death	Thou Will be done
Mark 11:25	Stand	Jerusalem by the withered fig tree	The disciples	Forgive others	Father forgives us
Numbers 16:22	Fell on their faces	Hill country of Canaan	Moses & Aaron	Mercy for Israelite Congregation	Congregation Spared [Not Korah]
2 Chronicles 7:1-3	Bowed down faces to the ground	The Altar of The Lord	Sons of Israel	Worship & giving praise	Praise to God
Psalms 134:	Lifting hands	House of the Lord	Pilgrims to the House of the Lord	Praise The Lord	Blessings from the Lord
1 Timothy 2:8	Lifting holy hands without wrath, without dissension	Ephesus	People in all places	Pray on behalf of all people	Acceptable in the sight of God, Who wants all to be saved
Psalms 4:4	Meditate on your bed	Place of danger (possibly a cave)	David	Deliverance & Safety	Peace – both lie down & sleep
Daniel 6:10-21	Kneeling	His house roof chamber	Daniel	Thanksgiving	Life spared in lion's den
1 Kings 19:4	Sitting	Under Juniper tree	Elijah	Fleeing from Jezebel, fear and wanting to die	Angel strengthened him with rest & food & water sustained him for 40 days and nights

1. Describe your position(s) of prayer.

2. Does position effect your praying?

IV. Pray without Ceasing – 1 Thessalonians[36]
- Know that this is a command.
- Know that this is a characteristic of Christian Living.
- Be willing to seek God first
- Pray whenever possible
- Pray whenever needed
- Pray whenever requested
- Have continuous fellowship with God throughout each day.
- Have an attitude of prayer:
    - Proper mental state toward God
    - Know that the Holy Spirit is our reference
    - Willingness to pray any time, anywhere, as the moment dictates
- Know that prayer makes the armor of God effective in defeating the enemy (Ephesians 6:18)
- Pray intercessory prayers

---

[36] Review 5:10-16.

- Pray:
    - Night watches – Psalm 63:6
    - Morning watches –Psalm 5:1-3
    - Always – Ephesians 6:18
- Request God's guidance through each aspect of your day
    - Pray as you reach each part of the day's agenda
    - Pray before unplanned events.
    - At the end of the day, check attitude for prayer.
- Jesus teaches on praying with persistence – Luke 18:1-4
    - Audience:
        - First parable – Audience is disciples
        - Second parable – Audience is group of self-righteous persons
    - Background – John 17
        - Jesus tells disciples importance of Faith (17:5)
        - Jesus tells of second coming and of Judgment of God
        - 17:34-36: Persons will be taken into judgment, some taken into the Kingdom
        - God's righteous judgment introduced.
        - Importance of faith stressed

- Characteristics:

Characteristics of Unrighteous Judge	Character of the Widow	Attributes of God, Just Judge
V2: Does not fear God Does not respect man Is impatient V3-4: Reluctant to give justice V4 Disobedient to O.T directive to care for widows	Persistent, O.T: Lacks social & economic position, particularly if no children (Book of Ruth) Dependent on family or the Church for sustenance	Merciful: Ruth 1:8, Hebrew 4:16, Romans 9:23 Protector of Widows, Exodus 22:20-24 Reliable: Numbers 23:19, Romans 2:3-4 Holy: Exodus 15:11 Righteous: Jeremiah 23:6 Love: 1 John 4:8-16 Eternal: Habakkuk 1:12 Longsuffering: Psalm 84:5 Just in rewards and punishments: Genesis 2:17, Romans 6:23
	She had need	

Discuss the outcome of the Widow's persistence. What is the application to prayer? Pharisee or Publicans, which is more likely to have an effective prayer life?

- Who were the Pharisees?
    - Mean separated ones.
    - Influential
    - Followed ritualistic Judaism
    - Antagonist of Christ, but many were converted.
    - Believers in Moses law
    - Dependent on Rabbis for interpretation of Scriptures.

- Who were the Publicans?
    - Tax collectors
    - Scorned by Israelites because served interest of Rome
    - Commended by Jesus because willing to believe
    - Willing to become humble
- Power of Perseverance
    - Read and discuss Psalm 1:1-6
    - 1 Thessalonians 5:17

- Application:
    - Faith leads to prayer.
    - God answers prayer when done in faith and in His will (James 1:6; 1 Peter 5:9)
    - Never give up hope
    - Those thought to be taken are ones who were steadfast.
    - Appearance, position are nothing.
    - Go to God in prayer believing, not justifying

How many commands have you followed?
How many of your prayers were for others? For self?

VI. The Ability to Communicate with the Supernatural:
- Biblical nature of man enables communication with the Father
    - Man composed of at least two components[37]
        - Dust
        - Breath of God
    - The material body made of dust
    - The body in its current form is not eternal[38]
    - The non-material part of man is Spirit.
        - The Spirit of God is in every man (Romans 8:9; Genesis 2:7)[39]
        - The Spirit of Christ is in the believer. (2 Corinthians 3:12-18)
    - Man's Spirit:
        - The heart is the intellectual part of man's spirit (Matthew 15:19-20)
        - Man's conscience is in the spiritual realm (Romans 2:15)
        - The depraved mind and lustful heart is void of the Spirit of Christ.
            - Man's spirit lacks wisdom of Spirit of Christ
            - Man's spirit darkened, has no conscience. (Romans 1:18-32[40]; Genesis 6:5)
        - Man's conscience is in the spiritual part of man. (Romans 2:15)
        - Man's lack of conscience is in the spiritual part of man. (Genesis 6:5)

---

[37] 2 Corinthians 5:1-10; Genesis 2:7; James 2:26; Job 34:14
[38] James 2:26; Job 10:9, 34:15; Psalm 104:29; Ecclesiastes 3:20, see chapter 1, pp
[39] The sin of Adam caused a separation of this Spirit from the Spirit of God, but the Spirit which enables life is present in all mankind. (Genesis 2:7)
[40] Romans 1:18-32 describes man's need for salvation, man's need for the Spirit of Christ.

- The Holy Spirit regenerates the spiritual part of man (2 Thessalonians 2:13)
  - Believer united to Christ through the baptism of the Holy Spirit[41]
  - The Holy Spirit regenerates the believer (John 3:3-6)
  - The believer is indwelled at the moment of belief. (Ephesians 1:13)
- One cannot be a Christian without the ministering of the Holy Spirit.
  - The Holy Spirit gives us authority in our communication with God.
  - The Holy Spirit gives us position in our communication with God.
    - Pray not as condemned but as children of God. (Romans 8:1,12-17)
    - Pray as joint heirs (legally adopted) with Jesus Christ (Romans 8:17)

VII. Know to Whom you are praying – Beware of the deception of Satan (Deuteronomy 18:10)
- Legacies from Old Testament Times:
  - Astrology
  - Satan worship
  - Transcendental Meditation
  - Yoga
  - Nature Worshippers
  - Voodoo
  - Card Readers
  - Psychics
  - Palm Readers
- The Occults
  - Subjecting supernatural power to human control
  - Concealed, not revealed

---

[41] Romans 6:3-4 and 1 Corinthians 12:13.

- Relating to supernatural agencies
- Jesus encountered the occult:
  - Mark 1:21-27 – unclean spirit of man in the synagogue
  - Mark 1:32-34 – They brought to Jesus those with unclean spirits
  - Mark 5- The demoniac of Gaderenes
- Persons maintaining covenant relationship with God will rely on God in all things.
- Sources not of God are from evil sources (Deuteronomy 18:10)
  - Diviners or soothsayers in Hellenistic – Roman religions
    - Told the inquirer what was expedient
    - Foretelling was conditional
    - The Mantes – replaced the Priests
  - Divination – A cloud reader
    - witchcraft – fortune teller
    - interprets omens – a spell caster
    - sorcerer – charmer of magic
    - spiritualist – consults the spirits
    - medium – wizard, calls up the dead for an abomination
  - Divination, a pagan parallel to prophesying (Vines)

THE MODEL PRAYER

I. "Pray, then, in this way: (Matthew 6:9 (NASB), **Our Father Who art in heaven, Hallowed be Thy name.**"
   - Who can address God as our Father?
   - Is there a difference between saying "Our Father", and saying "Our Creator?"
   - Only those who have been redeemed, reconciled back to God through Jesus Christ, can honestly say, "Our Father".[42]
   - To say our Father, 'Our' references the Disciples, therefore those who have been redeemed, who have redemption.

---

[42] Romans 8:12-17; Ephesians 1:3-12, with emphasis on verses 4-7.

- Our Father expresses a relationship we have with God.
- Jesus references God as Father, 8 times in this prayer.
- Our address to the Father is to reference His holiness, Who He is
    - The Man upstairs – No – Why?
    - The One Who watches over all – Close.

II. **Who Art in Heaven**
- In heaven, but close to His chosen through relationship
- Close yet separate from His creation.

III. **Hallowed be Thy Name**
- Αγιαζω, to make holy from hagios
- The opposite of common place
- Revelation of God's attributes
- Demonstration of reference and worship

IV. **"Thy kingdom come, Thy will be done, on earth as it is in heaven."** (Matthew 6:10 (NASB))
- The Kingdom references future promise of God
    - Matthew 3:2 (NASB), "Repent, for the Kingdom of Heaven is at hand." (Jesus).
    - Moral Kingdom
- **Thy Will be done** –θελημα
    - Sets priorities
    - 1 John 5:14 "And this is the confidence which we have before Him, that, if we ask anything according to His will, He hears us."
    - Demonstrates submissiveness
    - God's Will – Romans 12:2
        - Good – beneficial in effect
        - Acceptable – well pleasing
        - Perfect – complete
- **On earth as sit is in Heaven** – Recognizing God's sovereignty

V. **Give us this day our daily bread,** Matthew 6:12 (NASB) – Provisions for physical sustenance.

VI. **"And forgive us our Debts, as we also have forgiven our debtors."** (Matthew 6:12)
- Provisions for spiritual needs
- Moral debts
- Have forgiven, an act which has taken place, have been obedient (Matthew 5:23-24)
- Maintains relationship with Our Father
- Maintains fellowship with Our Father
- Our fellowship with God requires fellowship (forgiveness) with others.[43]

VII. **"And do not lead us into temptation, but deliver us from evil"**, Matthew 6:13.
- Our Father does not tempt us.[44]
- Paul's guidance: (Romans 7:19-25)
    - For the good I wish I do not do
    - I practice the very evil I do not wish to do
    - I find the principle that evil is present in me
    - I wish to do good
    - Wretched man am I
    - "Who will set me free from the body of this death?"
    - Thanks be to God.
- Acknowledge our weaknesses
- Acknowledge our fleshly battles
- The Greek form says: deliver from the evil **one, the devil is the tempter.**

---

[43] Matthew 6:14-15 (NASB), "For if you forgive men for their transgressions, your heavenly Father will also forgive you. "But if you do not forgive men, then your Father will not forgive your transgressions.

[44] James 1:13 (NASB), Let no one say when he is tempted, "I am being tempted by God:; for God cannot be tempted by evil, and He Himself does not tempt anyone. James 1:14: But each one is tempted when he is carried away and enticed by his own lust.

VIII. The Component parts of a Model prayer
- The Address – To Whom we are speaking
    o His Presence
    o Our relationship
- Reference – Recognition of His attributes
    o Knowing His closeness
    o Recognizing He is separate from us
    o Recognizing His position
- Reference to God's promises as **Statements of Fact – Truth**
- Setting the priorities of request to line up with God's Will
- Ensuring our relationship is in tact
- Ensuring that our fellowship is in tact

ROAD BLOCKS TO PRAYER

Sin.[45] (Jones, p. 39-47)
- Disobedience
    o Adam did not come out to converse with God in the cool of the evening following sin. He hid. (Genesis 3:8)
    o Our children seek to hide when they have disobeyed, we do the same.
    o It is the time we need to seek Him through Jesus Christ. (2 Corinthians 5:19)
- Not forgiving others (Matthew 6:14-15, Luke 6:37; Matthew 5:23-24)
- "Bitterness, anger, wrath…" (Ephesians 4:26-32)
- **List other items which are road blocks to a communication relationship with Our Father. Seek to see what the scriptures say:**
    o _____
    o _____
    o _____
    o _____

---

[45] Bishop Clifton Jones, *The Prayer Clinic Manual,* St. Louis: Hodale Press, Inc., 1997, p 39-47, provides 23 lessons on Prayer.

MINISTERING THROUGH PRAYER

James 5:16, "Therefore, confess your sins to one another, and pray for one another so that you may be healed. The effective prayer of a righteous man can accomplish much. (NASB)

I. Sharing with one another leads to prayer.[46] (Collins, p. 127-130)
   - We draw closer to those for whom we pray
   - Knowing someone is praying for you provides encouragement while we wait for God's answer

II. A ministering prayer – Intercessory prayer
   - Releases the person to God
   - Acknowledges we are not the resource for answering prayers

III. Situations of ministering prayers – form of sharing
   - Parent/child
   - Friends
   - Saints
   - Saints/Sinners
   - Friend/Foe

IV. Praying through scriptures aids sharing process (Collins, p. 127-130)
   - Assists in expressing thoughts
   - Opens persons for leading of Holy Spirit who intercedes for the believer

---

[46] Gary Collins, Ph.D. *Self-Talk, Imagery, and Prayer in Counseling,* Dallas: Word Publishing, 1986, p. 127-130.

SCRIPTURES WHICH HELP TO ENTER THE THRONE OF GRACE

CIRCUMSTANCES	**SCRIPTURES**
Sickness	Matthew 8:17
Prosperity	3 John 2
Blessings and curses	Deuteronomy 30:19
Faith	Mark 11:23, 24
Overcoming through salvation	Revelation 12:11
God's will	Isaiah 55:11
God's creativity attribute	Romans 5:11
Fear	Isaiah 41:10; 2 Timothy 1:7;
Coming near to God	John 14:27
Casting away problems	James 4:7-8
Restored health	1 Peter 5:7
Healing	Jeremiah 30:17
Forgiveness	Matthew 14:36; 15:30-31 Mark 11:25

BIBLIOGRAPHY AND SUGGESTED REFERENCES

Arthur, Kay. *Lord, I want to Know You.* Oregon. Multnomah Books, 1992.

Barker, Kenneth, Ed. *NIV Study bible, New International Version.* Grand Rapids, MI: Zondervan Publishing, 1985.

Christenson, Evelyn. *What Happens When Women Pray.* Colorado Springs, CO: Chariot Victor, 1991.

Collins, Gary. Ph.D, *Self-Talk, Imagery, and Prayer in* Counseling Dallas, TX: Word Publishing, 1986

Cornwall, Judson. *Praying The Scriptures.* Florida: Creation House, 1998.

Ingram, Jessica Kendall. *The Journey Inward, A Guide to Prayer & Reflection.* Detroit, MI: Journey Press, 1996.

Lea, Larry. *Releasing The Prayer Anointing.* Nashville, TN: Thomas Nelson Publishers, 1996, p1-12.

Smith, Alfred J. *Falling In Love With God.* Chicago, IL: Urban Ministries, 1997.

Tan, Siang-Yang and Gregg, Douglas H. *Disciplines of The Holy Spirit.* Grand Rapids, MI: Zondervan Publishing, 1997.

Thompson, Frank Charles, Ed. *The Thompson Chain-Reference Bible, New American Standard.* B.B. Kirkbridge Bible Company, 1983.

Vine, W.E., Unger, Merrill F., White, Jr. William. *Vine's Complete Expository Dictionary of Old and New Testament Words.* Nashville, TN: Thomas Nelson Publishers, 1985.

Walvoord, John F., Zuck, Roy B. *The Bible Knowledge Commentary, New Testament,* Colorado Springs, CO: Cook Communications, 1983.

BENEDICTION

Blessings to readers of this book:

In the name of the Father, Son and Holy Spirit, I wish you love, peace and abundant joy.

May the Lord bless and keep you in all of His Sovereignty. Giving to you wisdom, knowledge and understanding of the journey before you.

I pray that the grace of our Lord Jesus Christ be with you.

Amen!

Elder Arnoldine Lancaster

ABOUT THE AUTHOR

Brenda Simuel Jackson (BA, MA, Master of Divinity, Ph.D. Certified Biblical Counselor), is a born again Christian, affiliated with the Baptist Denomination. She is a member and Minister of New Prospect Missionary Baptist Church, and does ministry through BSJ Christian Seminars, Inc., a 501 (c3) Prison/Jail Ministry. She is a graduate of Wayne State University, and Moody Theological Seminary – Michigan, formerly Michigan Theological Seminary. She is a member of the pulpit, teaching, and prison ministries of her church.

Dr. Jackson has over thirty years of professional experience in human services, education administration, and management, as well as part-time collegiate instruction. She is currently a part-time faculty member of Wayne County Community College District. She has presented at Conferences of the American Association of Christian Counselors, local church women's retreats, mission programs, Christian Education Institutes, State Correctional Facilities, as well as Professional and Community Programs.

Dr. Jackson is a published writer who released her first book entitled, *A Journey of Redeeming Faith,* in April 2007. It was the first of four seminar compilations entitled, *Reflections on the Path to Wholeness.* The second in the series entitled, *Being Wonderfully Made"* was released April, 2008, and the third in the series, *Going Through",* was released in October, 2009. The current release, *Cross Roads,* is the last in this series. Dr. Jackson also hosted a radio broadcast, "God's Teaching Moments". Her Christian Journey includes short term outreach mission and prison ministry assignments in Japan, South Africa, Jamaica, and Ghana.

A native Detroiter, Dr. Jackson is a widow, a mother, grandmother, great grandmother, and ninth child of Willie and Lucy Simuel (both deceased). Dr. Jackson is a called minister of the Gospel. Dr. Jackson was licensed as a minister of the Gospel November 13, 2005, and she is currently pursuing certification as a Chaplain. Her vineyard is the prisons of the world.

Reflections on the Path to Wholeness: Vol 1
A Journey of Redeeming Faith

By Brenda S. Jackson, Ph.D.

Name _____

Address _____

City _____ State _____ Zip _____

Phone _____ Fax _____

Email _____

Quantity	
Price *(each)*	$9.99
Subtotal	
S & H *(each)*	$1.99
MI Tax 6%	
TOTAL	

METHOD OF PAYMENT:

☐ Check or Money Order (*Make payable to*: PriorityONE Publications)

☐ Visa ☐ Master Card ☐ American Express

Acct No. _____

Expiration Date (*mmyy*) _____

Signature _____

Mail your payment with this form to:
PriorityONE Publications
P. O. Box 725
Farmington, MI 48332
(800) 596-4490 – Toll Free
URL: http://www.p1pubs.com
Email: info@p1pubs.com

Reflections on the Path to Wholeness: Vol 2
Being *Wonderfully* Made

By Brenda S. Jackson, Ph.D.

Name _____

Address _____

City _____ State _____ Zip _____

Phone _____ Fax _____

Email _____

Quantity		
Price *(each)*		$11.99
Subtotal		
S & H *(each)*		$1.99
MI Tax 6%		
TOTAL		

METHOD OF PAYMENT:

☐ Check or Money Order (*Make payable to*: PriorityONE Publications)

☐ Visa   ☐ Master Card   ☐ American Express

Acct No. _____

Expiration Date *(mmyy)* _____

Signature _____

Mail your payment with this form to:
PriorityONE Publications
P. O. Box 725
Farmington, MI 48332
(800) 596-4490 – Toll Free
URL: http://www.p1pubs.com
Email: info@p1pubs.com

Reflections on the Path to Wholeness: Vol 3
Going Through

By Brenda S. Jackson, Ph.D.

Name _____

Address _____

City _____ State _____ Zip _____

Phone _____ Fax _____

Email _____

Quantity	
Price *(each)*	$11.99
Subtotal	
S & H *(each)*	$1.99
MI Tax 6%	
TOTAL	

METHOD OF PAYMENT:

☐ Check or Money Order (*Make payable to*: **PriorityONE Publications**)

☐ Visa   ☐ Master Card   ☐ American Express

Acct No. _____

Expiration Date (*mmyy*) _____

Signature _____

Mail your payment with this form to:
PriorityONE Publications
P. O. Box 725
Farmington, MI 48332
(800) 596-4490 – Toll Free
URL: http://www.p1pubs.com
Email: info@p1pubs.com

Reflections on the Path to Wholeness: Vol 4
CROSSROADS

By Brenda S. Jackson, Ph.D.

Address _____

City _____ State _____ Zip _____

Phone _____ Fax _____

Email _____

Quantity		
Price *(each)*		$11.99
Subtotal		
S & H *(each)*		$1.99
MI Tax 6%		
TOTAL		

METHOD OF PAYMENT:

☐ Check or Money Order (*Make payable to*: **PriorityONE Publications**)

☐ Visa   ☐ Master Card   ☐ American Express

Acct No. _____

Expiration Date (*mmyy*) _____

Signature _____

Mail your payment with this form to:
PriorityONE Publications
P. O. Box 725
Farmington, MI 48332
(800) 596-4490 – Toll Free
URL: http://www.p1pubs.com
Email: info@p1pubs.com

THE NEXT SERIES

The On-Going Struggle Vol. 1 & 2

```
            R
  C    R    O    S    S
            A
            D
            S
```

On-Going Struggle – Spiritual Warfare

Alone in a Fish Bowl

Fear & Faith

Parenting from a Prison Cell

Agape (Love)

You Shall Not Kill (Suicide) and Hope

Joy Comes in the Morning

The Reckening – Stewardship Appraisal

Talk to Me Interpersonal Communication

www.ingramcontent.com/pod-product-compliance
Lightning Source LLC
Chambersburg PA
CBHW052047070526
44584CB00017B/2091